Please Give a Devotion

a Devotion
FOR WOMEN'S GROUPS

Please Give a Devotion

FOR WOMEN'S GROUPS

Amy Bolding

BAKER BOOK HOUSE
Grand Rapids, Michigan

Library of Congress Catalog Card Number: 65-25478

Paperback edition issued
July 1976
ISBN: 0-8010-0583-3
Formerly published under the title,
Please Give a Devotion of Gladness

Copyright, 1965, by
Baker Book House Company

PHOTOLITHOPRINTED BY CUSHING - MALLOY, INC.
ANN ARBOR, MICHIGAN, UNITED STATES OF AMERICA
1976

This book is dedicated to my eight grandchildren who are my "Bits of Gladness": Rebecca Carpenter, Denise Carpenter, David Carpenter, Daniel Carpenter, Melonie Carpenter, Joel Greer, John Greer, and Sherri Bolding.

CONTENTS

BITS OF GLADNESS

Little bits of gladness
    Dropped into the soul,
In our times of madness,
    Help us keep control.

Little bits of gladness
    Brighten up our days,
Chase away our sadness
    With their sunny rays.

Little bits of gladness,
    Like the showers of rain,
Clear our thoughts of badness
    And bring hope again.

Little bits of gladness
    Strike a happy chord,
Bring a song from sadness,
    Help us serve the Lord.
                —J. T. Bolding

To Be Spent Brings
. . . Gladness

"And I will very gladly spend and be spent for you;
though the more abundantly I love you, the less I be
loved."—II Corinthians 12:15

THE SELF LOVER

The self-centered person, who looks for a glass,
Will seek out a mirror, to watch himself pass,
   Instead of a window toward other folk's needs,
   While he tells all the world of his own thrilling deeds.

He crashes the spotlight where'er it's turned on;
When other folk speak, he accords them a yawn;
   His own great importance impresses him much:
   Another's opinions? Why listen to such?

He knows all the answers and you ought to see
That he is important and smart as can be;
   But wrapped up in self, says the adage you read,
   He still makes a very small package indeed!
                 —J. T. Bolding

One hot day company came to our house. Two of the
visitors we knew and appreciated. The third, a maiden lady,
was a stranger to us.

9

The grandchildren rushed around and served cold drinks and candy, expecting to enjoy some talk on the junior level.

They were doomed to disappointment however. The visiting lady almost immediately began to tell us how important she was. She praised herself because she had a good job. She praised herself because she had accomplished a small feat in literature (collecting and publishing a small book of poems).

The children, disappointed, drifted out. My husband and I were obliged to sit and listen.

When the company finally left we immediately began to say, "Blessed is the man who tooteth his own horn, for if he tooteth it not, the same shall not be tooted."

She never knew how boring and ridiculous she seemed to us. If she had only been just a little bit interested in others we could have spent a pleasant half hour.

We are often unaware how much good we can accomplish by just a little time and interest spent for others.

Teach yourself to be glad for others.

Two boys, starting out to get into mischief one evening, stopped to speak to an old man sitting on his front lawn.

"Now you boys sit down and talk. I miss having young ones around." The older man asked the boys a question.

"What are you boys aiming to be?"

"I'd like to get on the railroad," one confessed.

"I wish I could farm," the other broke in.

"I was an engineer for thirty years," the retired one sighed. "You study hard in school then get on the railroad and build up."

"Do you think I could?"

"Sure you can. I wasn't half as smart as you are, and I got on. Have to work hard though."

The old man's wife came out and served cookies and lemonade. Dusk turned to darkness and still the three sat and talked. The old man told how a wealthy farmer started out hoeing cotton, "Just start at the bottom and go toward the top, son."

At ten o'clock the boys reluctantly dusted the grass off their trousers and arose to leave—for home.

"Did you know those boys?" the wife asked as the old man dressed for bed.

"Yep! Two boys needing a little encouragement."

"Those are two of the wildest boys in town."

"You don't say. I aim to help them be a good railroader and a farmer."

The old man did help just by spending time encouraging. The boys did get into the work they liked: someone believed they could, so they did. It takes so little effort to believe in people and it returns such great dividends.

Talking and living for self can become a bad habit. Sometimes a habit hard to break. Selfishness only pays in loneliness and repulsiveness.

Being glad to be spent for others pays in happiness and joy. A mother and father often do without things in order to provide opportunities for their children. They are glad to have the privilege of being spent for their children.

My mother sacrificed many things in order that my three younger sisters might study music. I have often heard her say: "I never sit in church and hear one of them sing or play but that I feel repaid a thousand times for all I did without to pay for their lessons."

I once read about a great church leader: "Unselfishness has marked his worthy course."

What a wonderful thing to have said about a person. How rich God's blessings must be for one who pressed forward to promote the kingdom unselfishly.

It is easy for some men to preach but hard for them to practice Christianity. It takes a sacrifice to practice.

A medical missionary, Dr. Mary King, wrote from China in 1935: "We can but praise the Lord for his abundant provision. . . . He sent us harder work and more of it."

You seldom hear a missionary speak who does not express grateful gladness at the opportunity to serve God.

11

E. Stanley Jones, said: "If Jesus Christ is not true, nothing matters. If Jesus Christ is true, nothing else matters." Let us determine like E. Stanley Jones to be one who is spent for God. Like Paul let us: "Very gladly spend and be spent for you."

MY FRIEND

There is a man who cares for me,
    'Tis easy to discern;
He asks about my family
    And voices his concern.

His interest is not merely feigned
    For when I talk with him,
His countenance does not grow pained,
    Nor eyes with far thought, dim.

I tell you that man's dear to me;
    He helps me on my way;
A better man I grow to be
    Through his concern each day.
                —J. T. Bolding

2

Cast Your Net for
. . . Gladness

". . . Who, when they have heard the word, immed-
iately receive it with gladness."—Mark 4:16
". . . Launch out into the deep, and let down your
nets for a draught."—Luke 5:4b

Most people are seeking something in this life. Most people
desire above all else to be content with life. I have known
many people who sought happiness in riches. Some spend
the best part of their lives seeking a fortune. When it is too
late they realize the empty loneliness of having only money.
Often too late they try to cast their nets on the other side.

A friend of ours was always bragging to us about being a
self-made man. He was a very wealthy man and had made
his fortune by his own cunning and hard work. Another
friend not quite so wealthy in land and houses would always take his field hands riding in his new car each year.

"We work hard for Mr. King to have his new car so he
lets us take a ride," the hands would tell their friends. Just
a little bit of gladness spread by a boss man but it paid off
in many ways. The first friend saw the days when his hands
all walked off the job and he lost a lot of money because he
had not taken time to be their friend as well as boss.

People often seek happiness in fame; some seek to find contentment in travel. Most common people seek happiness just one day at a time as they walk through life.

It is so refreshing to spend a few moments with a person who is content with his lot in life, a person who is thankful for God's daily blessings.

I grew up fifty-five miles from the great city of Dallas, Texas. Until I was eighteen years old I had never been to Dallas. Our own town seemed to be perfect to us. Children all rode in the family auto with the parents and if we wanted to go some place we walked to the park and back. Our life seemed quiet and peaceful. Two boys in a small town near ours were always discontented. They would sit under a shade tree in the square and tell all who would listen how they were going to see the world.

Money was very scarce in our part of the state but we bragged that it was the garden spot of the world for raising good beans, potatoes, tomatoes and all other food. The boys watched the trains come through town and decided to cast their net for fame and fortune on a boxcar. They had no idea how large the ocean of the world might be, but had to find out.

The two boxcar travelers, seeking happiness in travel, did just fine the first week. They had enough money to buy food that long. After their money ran out they started looking for work. Country boys of that day knew little about looking for work in a big city. Their nets seemed to be strangely empty.

One of the boys would tell their experiences at home later: "The day we got so hungry we had to go from door to door begging for food, I said, 'Let's go home.' "

The mothers told a different story. "We could not keep those two from talking, talking, about the big things they would do when they were old enough to get away from our small town."

"I guess home is a dull place to growing boys, but you

never saw such dirty hungry boys in your life as those two were when they came trudging home."

It is natural for the young to look at the grass on the other side of the fence and think it might be greener. It often is. Grass is not there for the taking; there must be work and direction of plans.

We find in the Scripture the Disciples had toiled all night and caught no fish. They were ready to give up the struggle. Something happened to change their plans. They saw Jesus! They were willing to follow Jesus' directions. When they followed Jesus' directions they caught more fish than they knew what to do with.

EMPTY NETS

Nets have taken nothing?
  All night long you've tried?
Hear the Saviour bidding,
  Try the other side.

Cast your net with gladness
  At the master's call;
He will give directions
  For a wondrous haul.

Launch out as He tells you;
  In His word abide,
Even when He orders,
  Try the other side.

You can trust His guiding
  And His power too;
When He says tell others—
  That is what to do.

You're to be a witness
  That, for men He died;
Hasten then to tell them
  He was crucified.

Tell them that the Saviour
  Will forgive their sin

If they'll only trust him,
And new life begin.
—J. T. Bolding

So many people feel they have failed in some undertaking because of the place they are in. That is not always true. Many fail because they have not seen Jesus. They have no directions from Him.

Jesus stands and waits at each heart's door, for people to let Him come in. Many discouraged people profess to know Christ but they fail to ask and follow His directions. The Disciples would have missed a great blessing, a great and profitable catch of fish, if they had refused to follow Christ's suggestion to "Launch out into the deep, and let down your nets for a draught."

We cannot be someone else; many of us cannot go some place else; many of us must use the same old net. What can we do? We have the same temptations day after day; we have the same personal faults; we have the same people to work with. There is a change we can make. We can look to the Master and ask His directions. We can tell him of our frustrations and toilings.

The two country boys who cast their nets in the ocean far from home (at least a few hundred miles; we never knew how far), came back to fish in the same waters but with contentment. Under Christ's direction the net will hold sufficient contentment and happiness if we let down for a draught.

Look to the Master, follow His directions and then put forth the effort to pull in the net. Your net will be filled with gladness and joy.

3

Fruitful Seasons Bring
. . . Gladness

"Nevertheless he left not himself without witness, in that he did good, and gave us rain from heaven, and fruitful seasons, filling our hearts with food and gladness."—Acts 14:17

When summer is almost over we begin pulling up dead flowers and clearing away our beds for winter. The farmers are busy harvesting their grain and cotton at this season. People are filled with gladness over the bountiful harvest.

Stop and think of all the long months of getting ready for the harvest! The soil must be prepared. The good Lord must send rain or snow. The seed must be planted. Then the crops start to grow.

Paul in the Scripture was speaking of the preparation Jesus made for a harvest. Do we just expect a great harvest of souls each time we have a service? More often than not we neglect the preparation of the soil, the sowing of the seed, the watering of the plants in order that we may have a great harvest.

Sometimes there are teachers of the Word who complain if they have to stay a little bit long at church services. They are cross if they fail to get away from the church quickly at noon. We are so busy about so many things. We want fruitful seasons but we fail to prepare for them.

On the Sabbath day we long to see an out-pouring of God's power. Through the week we are busy about many things and forget to sow the seed. We must seek the lost if we would harvest souls.

Harvest time on the farms is very exciting, with the many new machines to gather crops quickly and efficiently. Some of the farmers in the south have cotton harvesting machines capable of pulling a bale of cotton every few minutes. As a child I often picked cotton for school clothes. We would crawl along the rows pulling a heavy sack on our shoulders. Often the farmer would urge us to pick fast so he could get out a bale in two days. Harvesting methods have changed for farmers. Christ left us a method and it will not basically change. There will be no high-powered machinery developed to harvest souls of men.

One of my dear friends hires a full time maid to do her work. When the fall of year comes she reads an ad in the paper about fresh okra, tomatoes or peas for sale in the field. Off she goes in her big shiny car. She usually invites her neighbors to go with her. They go out in the field and gather all kinds of vegetables. Truly harvest time is fascinating. Those women have a wonderful time gathering things they could buy almost as cheaply without the trouble at the super-market.

The women going out to enjoy the harvest in the field remind me of churches. If we hear that a church is having a great harvest of souls at services, we make an effort to go. Why do people go in such great number to hear Billy Graham? They want to see a great harvest.

God wants us to have the joy of a bountiful harvest. Yet he wants us to prepare for the harvest. A woman in our church was ill in the hospital for weeks. There seemed no hope for her life. Churches asked special prayer for her. Through God's goodness she did get well. I happened to be in her home the day she arrived from the hospital. Friends were coming and going bringing food, flowers and tokens of love.

Her father arrived from California. He was old and feeble. He had made the long trip thinking she would not live; now he was seeing her at home and on the road to recovery. With tears streaming he watched people bringing in food. "Baby, you are reaping the harvest your mother sowed in this town."

"Tell me about it, daddy."

"Many times after she was going about her work in a wheel chair she would bake a pie or cake and ask me to take it to someone ill or with sorrow."

Listening to the old man I remembered a quotation: "Don't expect to enjoy the cream of life if you keep your milk of human kindness all bottled up."

As you go along life's highway, what kind of a harvest are you preparing for? What kind of seed are you sowing? There are seeds of prejudice, pride, cynicism, or just plain indifference.

The nation was shocked by the newspaper accounts of a girl in New York City who was stabbed to death while thirty-seven of her neighbors peeped from their windows and watched. They were too indifferent to call the police. One of those thirty-seven people might have been successful in driving away her murderer.

Are we guilty of peeping out the windows of life and being indifferent to the tragedy of lost people around us?

We think of those people who were so indifferent to the girl being murdered, as callous and cold. In our hearts we cry out, "Oh, how horrible!"

Day after day we see people under the influence of sin and Satan. We think how wasted their lives are. Do we take time to invite them to church, to tell them about God?

In Galatians 6:7-10 we read: "Be not deceived; God is not mocked: for whatsoever a man soweth, that shall he also reap . . . ."

Are we planting now for a glorious harvest in heaven?

Psalm 126:5, 6, reads as follows: "They that sow in tears shall reap in joy. He that goeth forth and weepeth, bearing precious seed, shall doubtless come again with rejoicing, bringing his sheaves with him."

WHERE WE ARE

We glamorize our mission work
  In lands across the sea;
We want to share the glad "good news"
  And missionaries be.

At least, a lot of us say so;
  But could this be pretense,
Since we neglect to tell our friend
  Across the backyard fence?

If we won't witness where we live,
  Can God use us afar?
Let's lift our eyes, the fields are white,
  And harvest ... where we are!
                    —J. T. Bolding

4

A Heart Filled with
. . . Gladness

"Go forth, O ye daughters of Zion, and behold King Solomon with the crown wherewith his mother crowned him in the day of his espousals, and in the day of the gladness of his heart."—Songs of Solomon 3:11

Way back in 1918 just after the close of World War I, our next door neighbor bought a car. How proudly he drove that car to the front of his home! All the neighbor children and most of their parents ran out to see and admire the new car. It was the first car most of us had ever been close to.

"Now all of you will get a chance to ride. Let's take four at a time besides me," the kind neighbor told us. The mothers scurried around getting hold of their offsprings. They would not think of letting their children ride unless they went along to hold them in tight.

When my turn to ride came I thought I would burst with happiness. My mother held me so closely I could not even peep over the side and see the wheels turning. I felt sure the whole town looked right at me as I rode by. I felt they were just green with envy.

Our whole neighborhood had a happy time that evening.

We talked about our feelings and whether we were scared or not and for one evening all the children stayed up late.

In our Scripture lesson when the daughters are told to go forth and see the young king, something exciting and different had happened. Solomon was coming home in a wooden chariot. Chariots were not common in Asiatic lands at that time. There were only pathways from town to town.

Solomon, the young and handsome king, was coming home in something new and different. His heart was filled with gladness, a crown was on his head.

So the women were to go and admire the king. Perhaps they had some of the same feelings we have in America when we hear our president will visit our town. We go to the street we think he will pass down, and often wait for hours. We are in a gay mood. We are happy to see the leader of our country.

How truly our hearts will be filled with gladness if we go forth to meet the king of our hearts. The ruler of our lives, our Lord Jesus Christ.

One summer we visited for a few hours on a farm in Alabama. There I met a little boy who impressed me as having a heart truly filled with gladness.

He knew nothing of the rush and hurry of the world away from his small community. He seemed perfectly satisfied as he told us about his world of pigs and pony, his school and friends.

"We just stay at home and enjoy it when we have company," he told us.

He was happy because he planned to be happy. Since receiving the letter telling of our coming he had planned to show us his pigs and pony. He had talked with his mother about what they would have in the way of refreshments. He was satisfied with his plans.

We have our wonderful Bible telling us of the coming of our king. I wonder if we are failing to make plans. We have the words over and over urging us to, "make ready." Are we planning with happy anticipation to be ready, to enjoy the great day? Do we have something to show our Master of the good we have accomplished?

An elderly friend plans a reunion of his family each year on the Fourth of July. Since he is the father of ten children and they are all married and have children, the crowd usually numbers around sixty or seventy people.

All year long that dear old man and his wife keep the reunion in mind. They raise a calf to be butchered. They feed a fat hog and have it roasted. Their cellar bulges with canned fruits and vegetables.

When the happy day arrives the clan gathers from far and near. The home to which they come is far out in the country. The house is much too small for so many but who minds eating out under the great oak trees on a hot summer day. There is much happiness in the great laughing crowd of kinspeople. They prepared to be happy and they expected to be happy at their reunion.

Christ will not come in a chariot made of wood, or in the latest model plane or car. Christ will come in glory. Glory too wonderful for us to even imagine.

> Oh that will be, glory for me, glory for me,
> When by His grace, I shall look on His face,
> That will be glory, be glory for me.

Happiness is a personal matter. You may choose to be sour. A young mother of three told me her experience with feeling badly. She was expecting a new baby and some Sunday mornings she really did not feel able to attend church services. She would mention her feelings at the breakfast table and one by one the husband and three children would say they were not feeling well either. The whole family would remain home, and poor sick mother waited on them as usual. The next time she woke up feeling ill she said not a word, just urged everyone to get dressed and eat their breakfast. When they were all ready for Sunday School she told them she would not go. They went on alone. They had always felt badly when they thought their mother did, so she kept it a secret.

So it is with happiness. We feel happy when we want to feel happy. We can sit and complain and drag the whole world down with us. We imagine many of our troubles.

Happiness is a by-product of other things. The person who is busy working at something he feels is worthwhile, finds his heart filled with happiness. The person who has a heart filled with love for others is an unselfish person. Unselfish people are as a rule happy people.

Happiness is also a by-product of friendship. One who has no time for friends usually leads a very lonely life.

Someone has aptly said, "The time we spend for serving others, and in there doing, serving God, is life's only lasting investment."

BITS OF GLADNESS

Little bits of gladness
  Scattered on the way
Cheer the weary trav'ler:
  Brighten up his day.

Little bits of gladness
  Shorten roads so long,
Tuning up the heart strings
  For a happy song.

Some folk bear great burdens
  'Til they're sick and blue;
Share your bits of gladness;
  Help the sunshine through.

Will you help men upward
  To the heights above,
And with bits of gladness
  Point them to God's love?

Will you be a blessing,
  Spreading o'er the land
Little bits of gladness
  From your helping hand?
        —J. T. Bolding

5

Christmas Means
. . . Gladness

"And thou shalt have joy and gladness; and many shall rejoice at his birth."—Luke 1:14

". . . Fear not: for behold, I bring you good tidings of great joy, which shall be to all people. For unto you is born this day in the city of David a Saviour, which is Christ the Lord."—Luke 2:10

The first Christmas came about because someone gave a gift of self. Christ came down to earth to provide salvation for us—the greatest gift of self ever known or that ever will be known.

Christmas should be a time of remembering. First of all we should remember our Lord and his gift to us. Christmas cannot truly come to our hearts unless Christ dwells therein. If we give Him thought and time during the holidays more of joy and happiness will be ours throughout the coming year.

Second, we need to remember at Christmastime that it is a time of giving—giving to those in real need, spiritually and physically. If we make a gift to missions or to our church, before we start our Christmas shopping, we are apt to be more careful what we spend on gifts for friends and family.

Christmas is a time of magic for children. They have faith

to believe all their dreams will come true. It should be a time, not of taking away the magic, but of teaching them why we have Christmas.

We once belonged to a church where a cross was placed on a table at the front of the church. The second Sunday in December a time was given for the people to pass by and place an offering for missions at the foot of the cross. It was a very quiet service but a very happy one. Some way we always felt we had put the right emphasis on Christmas and the getting ready for family celebrations seemed sweeter and easier after that.

Most families have some traditions they follow each year: hanging up stockings, making a certain kind of pudding or cake—things they enjoy doing and observing from year to year.

One of my friends found herself without funds at Christmastime. As she realized there would be no money for gifts, she felt sad and discouraged.

"I wish we could just skip over Christmas," she told her husband.

"Oh no, dear, Christmas is more than just giving expensive gifts. It is giving our love," her husband explained. "Let's make a list of those we want to give gifts to; then we can think of things we can make or do for them."

The list, when made, brought forth all kinds of possibilities. For the young couples with small children they prepared a hand printed card which read:

> "We will keep the children one night a month during the next year. You may go where you please those nights and come back when you please."

Needless to say the young couples were excited at the prospect of a free evening once a month. Some started collecting their gift immediately.

For the teen-agers on the list they prepared scrapbooks with all kinds of pointers for growing up and becoming well-adjusted. My friend clipped from all the magazines she could find to make those scrapbooks. She went to the public library and pored over books for teen-agers, making notes and putting them in the scrapbooks.

That was a happy group of youngsters as they glanced through the notebooks and saw what a lot of exciting information was compiled for them.

For some of the adults they made books of favorite recipes interspersed with poems clipped from papers and magazines.

My friends found a secret that Christmas, we should all learn and remember: "The gift without the giver is bare."

Our church places large boxes in the hallways before Christmas and even the smallest child is encouraged to bring a gift of non-perishable food to be placed in the boxes. Just before Christmas the food is divided and given to families over town who might be hungry during the winter weather. We find that giving in the name of the church helps people to realize that the churches represent God and that "God is love."

Our celebrations in our classes and clubs should not be just mere festivals of giving and receiving gifts. Programs which remind us why we celebrate Christmas should be given.

The greatest gift we can give to anyone is to tell him about Christ. If every real Christian determined to tell at least one person about Jesus during the month of December, think what a revival would spread over our land.

When you are about to be engulfed by the commercialism spread abroad at Christmastime, stop, look, and remember the cause of it all. Christmas comes when Christ dwells in our hearts.

SPIRIT OF CHRISTMAS

The beautiful spirit of Christmas
With joy is pervading the air
And spreading the warmth of its sunshine
To gladden men's hearts everywhere.

A miserly man sees a vision:
A needy, pale child, on his stroll;
His help opens eyes in pleased wonder,
And paints a bright spot on his soul.

'Twill place eager feet on dark stairways,
To leave heaping baskets of cheer,
For hearts all amazed at the goodness
Of those whose kind deeds make so dear.

This spirit of Christmas is prompting
Us all to be both good and kind
To those who are not blessed as we are,
If we would true happiness find.

In thousands of ways, this sweet spirit,
Is calling our hearts from the sod,
And bidding us keep up our service
To men as we live for our God.

—J. T. Bolding

6

Prayer Brings
. . . Gladness

*"The sacrifice of the wicked is an abomination to the
Lord: but the prayer of the upright is his delight."
—Proverbs 15:8
". . . God forbid that I should sin against the Lord in
ceasing to pray for you: but I will teach you the good
and the right way."—I Samuel 12:23*

As far back as I can remember I have known about prayer.
I am sure children do not know all about prayer, nor do
grownups; but children have faith. When I was a very small
child an older girl lived across the street from us. I thought
Alice was a very beautiful and wonderful person. One day
I heard my mother and father talking about Alice's father.
He was a very wicked man and when he was intoxicated
he would mistreat his family. My parents prayed for that
wicked man when we had our family prayers at night. I
loved Alice so much I would pray for her father sometimes
when I was alone. In that day and time it was stylish for
the furniture to be placed across the corners of the rooms.
We had an old fashioned organ. Mother left the organ just
a little out from the wall so a small child could go behind
and play dolls in the corner. Sometimes as I played behind

the organ I would talk to God and ask Him to make Alice's dad change. Then on Sunday when my father preached I would be very disappointed when the one for whom I had prayed did not come forward.

You might think a small child had no business bothering God over a drunkard. We moved away to another church and with the years I grew up. My parents went back to the community where Alice lived and they asked about all the people of years past. Yes, they asked about Alice; she was married and happy. Her father had given his heart to Christ and was living a better life.

More than forty years have passed since as a little child I prayed behind the organ. Now it is stylish for furniture to be flat against the walls and children have a hard time finding private places to play. But the same God who listened to a little child then hears those who call upon him today.

Prayer lifts heavy loads from our hearts. Prayer gives us courage to go on when the way looks dark. Prayer opens doors and melts hard hearts. Prayer changes lives and wins souls. Prayer brings response from God.

Samuel did not plan to stop praying for the Children of Israel just because they were wicked and sinful. Parents do not cease to pray for their wayward children. Pastors should not cease to pray for their church members, even when sometimes those members are cranky and hard to please.

Prayer is not a duty to be performed; it is a privilege to be used and enjoyed. It is the talking over of life's problems with one who has power to solve those problems.

Jesus never attempted to explain the mystery of prayer. He established a pattern and gave some rules. The mystery must be as your heart communes with one you honor and worship.

God delights in the prayer of the upright. Prayer is an expression of confidence in God. Prayer is an expression of our conscious need of God. Prayer is an act of obedience. Satan will keep us from praying if he can. When we neglect our prayer life we become weaker and weaker Christians.

Psalms 34:10, says "They that seek the Lord shall not want any good thing."

James 4:3, "Ye ask, and receive not, because ye ask amiss, that ye may spend it in your pleasures."

We are so busy going to meetings and doing things for our families, our classes, our churches, we neglect the greatest thing of all, prayer.

Jesus went aside to pray. If he felt a need for talking to God, how much more do we need that strengthening fellowship!

Ministers often make a mistake in thinking they must spend all the Prayer Meeting time teaching from some special passage. Prayer meeting is a good time to teach church members how to pray by letting them pray.

A teacher once asked a small boy why he thought the nine lepers did not thank Jesus for healing them. Said he, "I guess the first one took up all the time." The boy could have belonged to a church where the people are never given a chance to pray.

We should not put off all our prayers until the storms of life come along. If we pray constantly when the sun of life is shining then when the storms come along we will find it natural and easy to pray. I am persuaded God will find it natural and easy to hear our prayers when he is used to our voice.

We should never be like a little girl I saw in the grocery store. She ran away from her mother and began to pick at everything she could reach. She came to a beautiful display of pickles. "Mommie, I want some pickles," she began to call. Her mother busy filling the grocery basket paid no attention.

"I want pickles," became louder and louder.

The mother finally went to the child, "You are allergic to pickles; so we cannot buy them," she tried to explain.

The child screamed louder and louder, great tears rolled out of her eyes. She mussed up her hair, twisted her dress and in general put on a show.

She acted just like Christians do when they scream and

holler for God to send them some certain thing and never once say, "Thy will be done."

Greater achievements can be wrought by prayer than we have ever dreamed of. Why do we fail to pray?

If you have been neglecting your prayer life make some definite plans to change. Write out some verses of Scripture and some prayer plans and place them in a handy place, preferably your Bible.

Set a definite time to look at the paper and follow through on your prayer plans. Say you will set five three-minute periods at intervals during the day.

Read your Bible at least before one of your prayer periods and at other times try quoting some of God's promises. Matthew 7:7, 8, will be good to start with: "Ask, and it shall be given you; seek, and ye shall find; knock, and it shall be opened unto you; For every one that asketh receiveth; and he that seeketh findeth; and to him that knocketh it shall be opened."

If it is possible to have a time alone, pray aloud. I have talked to God many times as I drove to some appointment. Sometimes my old car made so much noise I guess I might just as well have prayed silently, but it did me good to voice my prayers.

Prayer is something we need to spend on others. Pray for your family, your pastor, your worst enemy, your friends. Praying for others helps us grow into bigger and better Christians.

Real prayer frees God to bring relief
From loads which weigh us down,
And give us strength to press along
As smiles replace a frown.

Real prayer frees God to light the way
In which we are to go,
To still the storm, supply our needs,
And take away our woe.

Real prayer releases God's great power,
    Within the heart and life,
To change defeat to victory
    And quiet inner strife.

Real prayer lets God work miracles,
    When human hope is dim,
And soften sinners hardened hearts
    As they are drawn to him.

                    —J. T. Bolding

7

Will Abundance Bring
. . . Gladness?

"Because thou servedst not the Lord thy God with
joyfulness, and with gladness of heart, for the abundance
of all things; Therefore shalt thou serve thine enemies
which the Lord shall send against thee, in hunger, and
in thirst, and in nakedness, and in want of all things;
and he shall put a yoke of iron upon thy neck, until
he have destroyed thee."—Deuteronomy 28:47, 48

For several years we have been going through a period
of great material abundance. Like the children of Israel God
has poured out His blessings upon us. Have we as Americans
and Christians been thankful for our blessings?

Many of us have forgotten what it is like to be in want.
We have new and comfortable church buildings. We have
nice homes and cars. Do we take all these things as a matter
of course, or do we thank God with hearts filled with joy
and gladness for His blessings?

I have a great weakness for pretty shoes. When I look into
my closet and see rows of bright, pretty slippers, sometimes
I remember my sophomore year in college. I had only one
pair of slippers. They had been bought with cotton-picking
money made on Saturdays. My mother had advised me to buy

a heavy pair of oxfords. The money was mine; so, foolish girl that I was, I bought flimsy dress shoes. We walked every place we went at school. Soon my pretty slippers had a hole in the soles. For over a month I had to put in pieces of cardboard each morning to keep from walking on the ground. Remembering those hard days I often breathe a prayer of thanks to God for his wonderful blessings.

Abundance brings with it great responsibilities. A woman whose husband had the best job in our little town, during the depression, was not thankful for her blessings. The pastor asked her to make an offering to the church.

"When I look at my husband's pay check," she told the pastor, "a tithe of it is too large an amount to give."

Today while many of the very poor people who sacrificed a dollar at a time to keep the little church going, are seeing better times, that woman lives a meager existence. Because she was not grateful for her blessings God took them away. Her once beautiful home is now owned by another. Her once very prosperous farm land is covered with flood waters. God took away her blessings because she was not true to her responsibilities in a time of abundance.

God expects people to be about the business of bringing in His kingdom.

During a revival in a rural community the pastor and evangelist went out on a Saturday to a large farm. They were looking for a hired hand who was not a Christian.

When they found him they told him, "We want you to attend our services tomorrow."

"I wish I could," he replied, "But during harvest we work all day Sunday."

"Then let us read some Scripture and pray with you now," the evangelist requested.

The owner of the farm had walked nearby. He spoke sharply to the young man and told him to get back to work.

The young fellow did not want to lose his job; so he said goodbye and walked away.

"We are too busy for visitors today," said the farmer. The

man turned away when the ministers would have told him about Jesus.

Like the man in the New Testament his barns were full but he had no time for something really worthwhile.

I am sure in His own time God said to that man, "This night shall thy soul be required of thee."

My husband and another minister had quite the opposite of this experience. They went to a busy downtown office to seek out a lost man. The head of the firm was very courteous.

"You gentlemen may use my office. I will send for him to come in."

The worker did not trust Christ that day but on the following Sabbath he and his whole family trusted Christ and united with the church.

The boss who was so kind as to let the ministers use his office will receive a blessing from God.

One of our responsibilities during our days of abundance is to share with others. Are we anxious to share our beautiful sanctuaries with every one, or do we gather our skirts about us and make people feel unwelcome if they are not on the same economic par with us.

For years I have worked with four-year-olds on Sunday nights. In the past few years we have moved from rooms in the basement of our church to lovely new departments opening on a nice playground.

One Sunday night two little girls wandering by drifted into our department. They were dirty, their hair uncombed. One child wore overalls. We placed them in the circle side by side with the other children.

When the children started singing the two visitors sat spellbound. Their faces were transfixed.

The circle leader, noticing the joy and interest on the little ones faces had the children sing many more songs than usual.

Seeking to find more about them, we discovered they were children neglected by parents, left here and there with relatives.

36

As we shared the abundance of God's love with those two little ones, we found it was not wasted on their hungry hearts. The following verse was written many years ago by a Mrs. Charles.

For the heart grows rich in giving:
   All its wealth is living grain;
Seeds which mildew in the garner,
   Scattered, fill with gold the plain.

Is thy burden hard and heavy?
   Do thy steps drag wearily?
Help to bear thy brother's burden;
   God will bear both it and thee.

Is the heart a well left empty?
   None but God its void can fill;
Nothing but a ceaseless fountain
   Can its ceaseless longings still.

Is the heart a living power?
   Self-entwined its strength sinks low;
It can only live in loving,
   And by serving love will grow.

8

Open the Gate for
. . . Gladness

"And when she knew Peter's voice, she opened not the gate for gladness, but ran in and told how Peter stood before the gate.—Acts 12:4

Have you ever been so filled with happiness that you did something foolish? Rhoda was.

A young father I knew went to the hospital to wait while his wife was in the delivery room. After a long wait the nurse came to the door and spoke to him, "You have twin boys."

The father was so excited he jumped up and rushed down to the heart of town to tell all his friends and co-workers.

The thought that his wife or the twins might not be doing well never occurred to him, he was just so happy he had to let his world know about it.

"How is your wife? Are the babies all right?" His boss asked when told the news.

"Oh! I never thought of that. They have just got to be fine. I was just so happy." He rushed back to the hospital.

We have all known foolish moments of great joy.

Peter had been asleep between two guards; he was bound with chains. Perhaps he dreamed fitfully of how James had been killed. He was himself, most likely to be killed after the Easter holidays.

> His dream was changed—the tyrant's voice
> Calls to the last of glorious deeds;
> But as he rises to rejoice,
> Not Herod, but an angel leads.

The people in the church had not ceased to pray for their beloved Peter. Now God answered their prayers. Even as they prayed the little girl in the home went to answer a summons at the gate.

When she saw the one for whom they prayed, standing outside the gate, she rushed away to tell the others. Perhaps the whole group rushed back to the gate to rejoice and welcome Peter in.

In order to open the gates of life for gladness to come in, we must first of all have an abiding trust in Christ our Saviour.

We must, like Paul, "Know whom I have believed and am persuaded that he is able to keep that which I have committed unto him against that day."

Frederick Douglas, who lived in the days of slavery, and was a slave, wrote like this:

"When I was a slave I prayed earnestly for freedom and made no attempt to gain it, and I got no response, but when I began to pray with my legs, my prayers began to be answered."

Douglas after he gained his freedom, by escaping, made a contribution to his people by writing and speaking on the abolition of slavery.

We have only one life to live. We can live behind a wall of selfishness, covetousness, or many other things with which we build walls. The best way to live is to open the gates of those self-made walls and let gladness come in.

When we trust Christ, and the gladness of being children of the King comes into our hearts, we receive some privileges. Prayer is a great gift to those who trust Christ.

Prayer brings wide the gate of gladness, filling us with a sense of peace and quiet.

O make me patient, Lord,
Patient in daily cares;
Keep me from thoughtless words,
That slip out unawares.
And help me, Lord, I pray,
Still nearer thee to live
And as I journey on,
More of thy presence give.
—Anonymous

So if you would open the gates of gladness and live a joyous, happy life, you need to remember the following:

Christ must be first in your heart and life.

You must spend time in prayer and trust God for the best answers.

We must have patience with the faults of those about us.

We must be good at forgetting the wrongs and faithful to remember the blessings of our daily lives.

Gates of gladness never open while hearts are filled with selfishness, unkindness, ignorance and covetousness.

HOW TO BE HAPPY

Are you almost disgusted with life, little man?
I'll tell you a wonderful trick
That will bring you contentment, if anything can,
Do something for somebody, quick!

Are you awfully tired with play, little girl?
Wearied, discouraged, and sick—
I'll tell you the loveliest game in the world,
Do something for somebody, quick!

Though it rains, like the rain of the flood, little man,
And the clouds are forbidding and thick,
You can make the sunshine in your soul, little man,
Do something for somebody, quick!

40

Though the sun is like brass overhead, little girl,
And the walks like a well-heated brick,
And our earthly affairs in a terrible whirl,
Do something for somebody, quick!

—Unknown

9

Lifted Shades Bring
. . . Gladness

"Say not ye, There are yet four months, and then cometh harvest? Behold, I say unto you, Lift up your eyes and look on the fields; for they are white already to harvest."—John 4:35

A man riding along the highway in a fast motor car, had all the windows up, the radio playing and his mind on the problems of his business. A man standing on the side of the road near a wrecked auto waved to him and called out begging him to stop and give assistance. The man in the car went merrily on down the road. The one begging for help went back to the side of his injured wife, who was bleeding to death.

If the man driving the car, listening to music and working on his own problems, had only lifted his eyes and looked to the man needing help, he might have rushed the woman to the hospital and saved her life. When I heard the woman's husband tell how he had to watch her die when she could have been saved I thought: "How selfish, how cruel!"

Yet are we not daily losing some blessing of helping others because we do not lift the shades and look about us for those in need of our help?

For every person in this world there is some special task

to perform. It may be a lowly one in a small place but it is his task. If he fails to do his part some good for the world will be lost.

A frail little mother wrote me a letter. She lamented the fact that by the time she kept her home clean and washed and ironed for her husband and two small children she had no time for creative work. In answering I tried to make her see she was doing the greatest work in the world when she trained fine children and kept her home happy.

> Others may do a greater work,
> But you have your part to do;
> And no one in all God's heritage
> Can do it so well as you.
> —Selected

In the Old Testament we have the story of Abraham pitching his tent on the plains of Mamre. Then he sat in the tent door to look out at his world. If the sun was shining extra hot I expect he lifted the sides of the tent for the breeze to blow through. In Genesis 18, we have the story. As Abraham sat looking over the plain he saw three men coming. He ran to meet those men. They brought a blessing to him.

The world today is waiting for more people who will lift the shades of life and look for opportunities—people who will run to meet life and give their best to it. I know a man who has a good job in a bakery. He is supervisor over several men and a lot of equipment. He started working after school when he was twelve years old. The owner of the bakery loves him like a son. Why? He has always been willing to lift the shades and look around to see what needed doing.

Too many people are riding through life with the windows up, and the radio going, their minds on nothing except quitting time and pay day.

Youth today can look on horizons to the four corners of the world. The responsibility of the older generation is to help them lift the shades of their daily lives and look for those who stand helplessly and beg for attention.

Many of the young people who have gone to work in the Peace Corps have come home with broader vision. They have a better insight into the problems of the world. They have a greater appreciation for the many advantages and blessings Americans enjoy.

At a club meeting I sat by a woman well past middle age. "How can I serve the world?" she asked.

"Lift the shades and look around you. There is much to do," I replied.

"Oh, I don't mean just helping hungry people or taking some half-worn-out clothes to those who are destitute. I want to do something spectacular."

I could not, at that time, remind her that the one who lived the most spectacular life said, "Inasmuch as ye have done it unto one of the least of these my brethren, ye have done it unto me" (Matthew 25:40).

We are often afraid to lift the shades on friendship. We just don't care to be friends with that new family on the block. Their children might ask a favor or run across our flower beds. How many blessings we miss because we do not make friends with many people!

One of my dearest friends belongs to a different denomination from mine. We never argue over our beliefs. I respect her and she does the same for me. If I lowered the shades and refused to have her for a friend because she does not see eye to eye, I would miss a great blessing.

I heard of a man in this day of world travelers who took a tour of Europe. He would not go with any of his party to see the great cathedrals. He missed seeing many of the great works of art. Why?

"They would not visit my church if they were in my town and so I don't intend to visit theirs."

He had his shades pulled down tight. We must keep our shades of knowledge lifted high. There is always something new to learn. Look at many of the great discoveries of the world: electricity, automobiles, planes, telephone. What if

Edison, Ford and the others had said, "I will not seek this knowledge although I believe there is a better way."

A small boy worked all morning under a peach tree. At noon he urged his busy mother to come and see his invention. She found a large number of bottles filled partly with water and hanging from a low limb of the tree. The child played a tune on the bottles with a stick. The mother could have pulled down the shades and acted cross but instead she sat still and listened. She bragged about the music. Years later her son paid part of his way through college by playing in the band. He was encouraged to develop his love for music.

People who lift the shades of life and look to see where they may serve, where they may make friends, where they may spread love, where find knowledge, those are the people who find happiness.

SHOW OTHERS WHAT JESUS CAN DO

Prove by the smile on your face ev'ry day,
  Prove by the wisdom He gives when you pray,
Prove to the world there's no other way,
  Show others what Jesus can do.

Prove by the burden you're willing to bear,
  Prove by the comfort and cheer which you share,
Prove in His service you'll go anywhere,
  Show others what Jesus can do.

Prove by each act you're a child of the king,
  Prove that you fear neither life nor death's sting,
Prove by your faith till in glory you sing,
  Show others what Jesus can do.

Show others what Jesus can do,
  Thro' His grace from above,
Give the message of love,
  And show others what Jesus can do.
                                    —Scott Lawrence

10

Thanksgiving
. . . Gladness

"Light is sown for the righteous and gladness for the
upright in heart."—Psalm 97:11
"Offer unto God thanksgiving."—Psalm 50:14a

Thanksgiving is something so big we cannot put it in the
month of November and tie it up with a bow. We must open
the package of thanksgiving and let it fill the atmosphere of
our whole year.

> 'Tis the season of Thanksgiving
> For abundant harvests near
> But so much we are receiving
> From our blessed Lord, it's clear,
> That in gratitude, our living
> Should give thanks all through the year.
> —J. T. Bolding

From the first Thanksgiving Day in 1621 the idea of the
special day was to give thanks to God for his bountiful harvest. The real spirit of true thanksgiving as it spills over into
every day of life is expressed in I Thessalonians 5:18, "In
everything give thanks: for this is the will of God in Christ
Jesus concerning you."

If we believe on Jesus and let him direct our lives, we have something to be thankful for each day.

When we think of new dimensions we might give Thanksgiving, our thoughts turn first to those we love. After we have given thanks to our God for them, there are others we might think about with thanksgiving.

Wouldn't it help our lawmakers to strive more for the right if many, many Christians wrote a letter thanking them for holding office, and for trying to keep our nation free?

Wouldn't your pastor or Sunday School teacher have a happier day if you called and told them how much you appreciated their work? You might try sending them a little note of appreciation.

Really to give Thanksgiving a new dimension we need to draw our thoughts away from our own cozy happy homes and take some food or clothing to a family less fortunate than we.

Families will find a great blessing if they take a few moments around Thanksgiving time, to discuss their blessings and perhaps make a list as they have family devotions. Perhaps the parents will name blessings the children merely took for granted. The children may be thankful for things the parents did not realize were considered precious. Thanksgiving will have new dimensions if we spend more time being aware of our blessings and less hurry and scurry over cooking a large meal.

A small child heard the teacher at Sunday School talk about things for which we should be glad and thankful. When he went home his mother was busy cooking and merely said hello. He went out on the steps and sat so the November sun would warm his back.

"What are you doing Jimmy?" his mother called.

"I am just being glad with the sun," he answered.

Do you ever take time just to be glad with the sun?

We want our Thanksgiving to have dimensions big enough to carry us through trouble and sorrow. David thanked God for delivering him from his distress and sorrow. We should thank God for being with us when sad and trying times come. If we are his children he is with us to comfort and heal.

We should offer sympathy and help to those who are going through difficulties. We show gratitude to God for his blessings when we offer comfort and help to others.

We can show gratitude and thanksgiving by using kind words, which like the smell of turkey and dressing, give an aroma of happy inspiration.

Gratitude for our blessings will speak loudly; the absence of gratitude will speak even more loudly. Gratitude seems such a small thing. Yet it is a jewel shining brightly to make people more lovable and happy. As parents we need to teach our children the grace of gratitude.

A lady and her teen-age son came to see me. They were driving a very expensive new car. I had never been in a car so nice. They asked me to take a ride. The ride was a lot of fun but the nicest thing about it was when the mother said to her son, "We are so glad we have such a wonderful daddy to buy nice things for us."

Just simple words, but as that young man has grown into manhood I have noticed what a wonderful spirit of love and gratitude he had toward his daddy who happens to be his stepfather. His own father died when he was six months old.

A lady in our territory was interviewed by a reporter on her ninety-seventh birthday. She was asked to tell some of her early experiences in dry West Texas.

She told of a seventeen day trip by covered wagon. When at last they reached the place they were going to homestead she climbed down from the wagon and looked around her. "I found a world of grass and sky. To me this was the 'Promised Land.'" All her words were words of thanksgiving for the privileges she had enjoyed making a home in a barren land. No word of complaint about water being so scarce, food very hard to get and the bitter cold blizzards in winter. She closed her interview by saying, "I have had lots of troubles but, Thank God, they have all been decent ones."

Christians should take stock and be sure they have the pro-

48

per dimensions on their Thanksgiving. There should be no room or time for complaints. If we are inclined to complain, quote Romans 8:28.

THANKS, LORD

I thank Thee, Lord, for eyes to see,
The beauty of each thriving tree.

I thank Thee, Lord, for nose to smell,
Beautiful flowers I love so well.

I thank Thee, Lord, for ears to hear,
The voice of those I love so dear.

I thank Thee, Lord, for hands to work.
I pray Thee, Lord, they never shirk.

I thank Thee, Lord, for feet to walk,
And for a tongue that I may talk.

I thank Thee, Lord, for Thy creation,
But I thank Thee most for my salvation.
—Mary M. Baker

11

Hearing Joy and
. . . Gladness

*"Make me to hear joy and gladness . . . . Create in me
a clean heart, O God; and renew a right spirit within
me."—Psalm 51:8, 10*

To a young mother holding close her first born baby, the
sweet little coo of her baby is a sound to bring gladness. To
young lovers the words, "I love you" bring gladness.

Have you ever been privileged to see high school or college
graduates when their name was called to walk forth and receive their diploma? To them the calling of their name was a
sound of gladness. That name was called only after years
of hard study and constant striving to learn the required sub-
jects.

To the parents of the graduates it was a sound of joy and
gladness to know their years of expense were being rewarded.

One spring I was standing in our local college book store.
Three boys were discussing their coming graduation. They
were excited and happy over the places where they were going
to work. A fourth boy entered the store. The three happy
boys called to him.

"Where are you going after graduation?" they asked him.

"I had signed a contract to work for a big company." He sounded so sad. "Today I found I cannot graduate. I failed one of my courses."

The boy was young and I hope he was made of the stuff which would cause him to take the course over and try again.

God knows our human weaknesses and in His mercy and wisdom He planned a way for us to receive forgiveness for our sins.

The words found in John 3:16, ". . . whosoever believeth on Him might have everlasting life," should be words of joy to all who believe.

If we want to hear the sounds of joy and gladness, then we must play the music of life which will bring happiness.

When David wrote the fifty-first Psalm, he was a great king. It was not easy for him to acknowledge his sins and ask forgiveness. Yet he did ask forgiveness. He asked God to make him hear sounds of joy and gladness.

A popular movie and T.V. star wrote a story about meeting his father after many years. The father had deserted his wife and children when they needed him most. Through the years the son had thought of all the unkind things he would like to say to his father, if ever the opportunity came. Then one day his phone rang and the voice on the other end was that of the star's once loved father. The father acknowledged his sins and asked the son to forgive him. That famous young man forgot all the ugly things he had planned to say. He was overcome with joy. He was happy just to know his father was still alive and still loved his son.

The Christian can hear sounds of gladness in unexpected places. If they are about the Master's business, the sweetest sound will be, "Well done thou good and faithful servant."

> Let us gather up the sunbeams
>   Lying all around our path;
> Let us keep the wheat and roses,
>   Casting out the thorns and chaff;

Let us find our sweetest comfort
In the blessings of today,
With a patient hand removing
All the briars from our way.
—Selected

Once at a student night program I watched as more than
fifty young people marched down the aisle of our church. The
lights were off and the young folks were carrying small
torches. As they marched they sang, "Stand Up, Stand Up
for Jesus."

I will always remember the impression that beautiful music
made on me. I wanted to get up and go out to work for
Jesus. No great choir could have sounded any sweeter to me
than those Christian young people singing for Jesus.

Hearing the voice of my husband after he had been away
on the battle front during World War II was one of life's
sweetest moments. Just to know he was back in the States,
was coming home. I don't think either of us said many words
on that phone but even the tears had a happy sound.

If we want to hear happy sounds we must sing happy useful
songs. We sing happy songs in life when we plan life that
way. There will come difficult times when the music seems
to be in a minor key but the person trusting in God and
living for him will find those minor notes only serve to make
the happy days sweeter.

Birds are very scarce in our part of the state. Yet we have a
mockingbird who nests near our yard each summer. We enjoy
being awakened each morning by the bird's singing. To en-
tice the bird to stay with us we bought a bird bath. We also
put pieces of dried bread near the bird bath. It is not much
trouble to do these little things, yet it assures us of sweet
music.

Just make doing nice things a habit of life and when the
music comes back from them you will have a nice surprise.
It does come back pressed down and running over.

HAPPINESS

Are you struggling to be happy
  As along your way you go?
If you're running into problems,
  There's a thing you ought to know.

Happiness is not a garment
  Which you don or doff at will,
And you likely cannot buy it
  Though you've money in your till.

It's a certain brand of thinking;
  It's an attitude of mind;
It's a thoughtfulness of others
  Which leaves selfishness behind.

If you make another happy,
  You are planting wondrous seed
Which may multiply his blessings
  And fulfill your own deep need.

              —J. T. Bolding

12

Stones of Memorial Bring
. . . Gladness

"That this may be a sign among you, that when your children ask their fathers in the time to come, saying, What mean ye by these stones?"—Joshua 4:6

In Northwest Georgia, near Atlanta, there is a partly completed Stone Mountain Memorial to the Confederacy. In South Dakota in the Mount Rushmore National Memorial we find the figures of presidents Washington, Jefferson, Lincoln, and Theodore Roosevelt. These figures have been carved over a long period of time by a sculptor, Gutzon Borglum. Whether you travel to Georgia or South Dakota, if your children see the impressive memorials (not yet complete), they will ask some questions. Why those particular men? Why in this certain place? How could men carve the granite?

In our wonderful homeland where everything is made easy for us, the children will probably have gotten literature at the information desk and tell you all about the memorials before you can get your bi-focals adjusted for a good look.

As Americans we are proud of our traditions. We are proud of our heros. Organizations and the government have spent great amounts of money in order to establish memorials and historic markers.

God told the Children of Israel to make a memorial with twelve stones, representing the twelve tribes. All the tribes of Israel had passed over Jordon on dry ground. They were to take the stones from the river bed. Those twelve stones were the visible proof of the miracle. They were not to represent the power of Joshua, but the mercies of God in bringing them to the promised land.

In the years and ages to follow the people were to explain the memorial to their children in order that they too might know of God's miracles and mercy.

A philosopher called Glover has said: "We owe it to ourselves to remember all God's benefits, for the recollection of them is green pastures and still waters when we are weak."

Joubert said: "Monuments are the grappling irons that bind one generation to another."

All over our beautiful America we have bronze markers and stone markers, telling of historical events. We love to take trips over the land and stop to read these markers. When we visit in foreign lands we take time to look at the monuments and statues they have erected to the memory of their great.

When our loved one dies we place the most beautiful marker we can afford over his grave.

As long as there are people on the earth there will be tradition and memorials. Many people have little family traditions which they treasure. Many villages and towns have different types of yearly celebrations they carry on in memory of their founding fathers. Our nation has the practice of celebrating the Fourth of July, the day we remember the cost of our freedom.

Christianity has a heritage of many great leaders, among whom are Martin Luther, John Knox, Charles and John Wesley, Luther Rice and William Carey. Time or space would not allow us to name even a fraction of the great men in the religious world to whom we have erected memorials.

When our children ask us the meaning of the traditions of our world, are we able to tell them?

We can better evaluate the present if we know some of the hardships of the past. We should ever be grateful for those who made straight the way before us.

The stones made into a memorial by the Israelites were to remind them of God's mighty power. Are we guilty of waiting and looking for some mighty pile of stones before we remember God's power? The stones were to remind them of God's love for his people. Can we fail to believe in that love when we look about and see his wonders each day? The stones were to remind them of God's mercies. Let us be alert to recognize God's mercies each day.

One of my favorite preachers very often says, "If I were in God's place, I am sure I would not be so patient with my mistakes."

Then the stones were to remind the people to teach their children of God and his mighty works.

A friend of mine was teaching a class of college boys and girls. She asked the question, "What do you think God is like?"

"He seems like a ghost to me," from a freshman.

What would your child answer? Are we true to our heritage as we teach our children? Some parents take more pains teaching their children polite manners than they take to teach about the one who gave them life.

Are you building an altar of remembrance in your life? We need to place on the foundation of our memorial a large stone of knowledge, declaring that God is our Creator, our Sovereign King.

Another great stone is a realization that Jesus Christ is the door to eternal life, the way to the Father.

STONES

There are stones raised to remind us
Of God's providential care;
And he asks us to remember
Our salvation hopes to share.

Do you have to be reminded
To tell folk of Calvary,
And that they may have salvation
As a gift, from him, "for free"?
—J. T. Bolding

A bright shining stone of memory should be for the Bible, which is our guide book, our inspiration, our Word from God. The principles in the Bible will direct us in the right and happy way to live.

Then place a stone for the Holy Spirit, sent to be our Comfortor, to abide in the hearts of the redeemed. Our children need to know and understand what these memorial stones stand for.

There must be a stone to remind us that all men are sinful; that all have come short of God's perfection. Sin keeps us from God; sin is against our Heavenly Father. Escape from the condemnation of sin to the forgiveness of God is through faith in Jesus Christ, who becomes our substitute and, thereby, our Saviour.

We might stack up two beautiful twin stones to represent the cross and salvation. The cross of Christ represents, or reveals His great love for sinners. Salvation can only be ours as we believe Christ died for our sins upon the cross, that he gives us new life when we believe in him as our atonement for our sins.

Then there should be some stones to remind us there is work yet to be done—stones representing missions, evangelism, service for God. Then let there be one for our church, God's established body, through which we can help tell more of the world about Jesus.

What mean these stones? Are we sure we know? Are we faithfully telling the next generation?

MONUMENT

Sometimes men use a marble shaft
To mark a great event,

And also oftentimes erect
O'er graves a monument.

Since our dull minds must be refreshed,
God brings into our view
Reminders of his providence
And love each day, anew.

So Jesus left a monument
To stir our memories dim,
And now the Supper of our Lord
Reminds us all of Him.

—J. T. Bolding

13

Chosen with
. . . Gladness

"And he brought forth his people with joy, and his chosen with gladness."—Psalm 105:43

Going up to an attractive stranger after church services one Sunday, I introduced myself. As we chatted for a moment, a pretty little black haired girl came running up to the lady and grasped her hand.

"This is my little daughter, Susie," she told me.

"I'm a chosen one!" the child looked at me with big beautiful brown eyes. "Some people just take any baby God sends but my mommie went to a big baby home and chose me."

Unconsciously the mother has pulled the little one closer to her and looked at her with much fondness.

"Yes, we could have picked many others, boys and girls, but we liked Susie best of all."

How happy the mother and daughter were to have each other.

Not all the people I know are as happy with their adopted children as that new friend seemed to be. I knew a sweet Christian couple who adopted a child and over indulged her about everything. When she grew older she was constantly causing them trouble and heartache. Perhaps their choice was all right. Maybe it was their method of handling that choice. At any rate, to be chosen brings responsibilities for both the chooser and the one chosen.

God has chosen us. He gave us a divine leader. Because we are chosen we have obligations to live for Christ. Christ sacrificed his life for us. We should be willing to live our life for him.

In Deuteronomy 7:6, 7, 8, we read that God chose the children of Abraham because he loved them. We make many choices because we love someone. Our choices can bring us happiness or sorrow depending on whether they are right or wrong.

Our whole lives from the cradle to the grave are made up of choices. We chose companions; we choose schools; we choose jobs; we choose to be good or evil.

We have read and heard so many heartbreaking stories about people who wanted freedom—people who were willing to risk their lives for freedom. Not long ago two women spoke at a mission meeting. They were refugees from their own country. One told us that although they had been quite wealthy in their own land their children had to send them money for passage to freedom. Everything they had spent their lives getting had to be left behind. Yet as they talked I felt they had made a right choice. Their three sons had been in America several years and longed to have their parents with them. The sons needed the love and guidance of parents. The sacrifice of leaving worldly possessions behind was forgotten when they felt the arms of three strong sons around them.

To choose the things in life which will bring satisfaction and happiness we need a great deal of guidance. We would not think of starting on a cross-country trip without some type of map. We find, as children, our parents usually help us make right and wrong choices. After we grow older we begin to wonder how best to make decisions.

The greatest decision a person can make is the decision to give his heart to Christ. After that choice has been made we

60

have the Holy Spirit to guide us. We must seek to find God's choice for our life. How can we find God's will for us? We can build our lives around the word, "service." We can work and also relax in a spirit of love and service for others. When we are living to serve, God opens the way before us and guides our choices.

I know a sweet Christian family who face the problem of tithing. Like other young couples they were paying on a home, on a washing machine and probably other things. It would have been easy to put off giving to their church until some other time.

"We will pay our tithe first and live on the rest." They did not make this choice easily, but with painful searching and prayer.

When they had been married a few years and finances seemed to be the biggest problem, God opened the windows of heaven and poured out for them a great blessing. They had no rich relatives to die and leave a fortune. God just simply opened up a job for the young man that paid twice what his job paid when he started tithing.

"We have never regretted our decision to tithe," the young mother told me. They still have to watch their pennies but they know the Heavenly Father is watching over them, and they have the joy of feeling chosen and cared for.

Life is a personal matter. No one can live it for you. You must live life as you choose. Whether you are happy or not will depend upon your choices.

When my mother was a little girl, dolls were very scarce. The only doll she and her older sister had was one made of corncobs and dressed in pieces of old clothes. An uncle came from another state. He brought with him a beautiful china head doll. The little girls had never seen a boughten doll before. They were fascinated with such a wonderful toy. When the uncle started to leave he gave the doll to the older sister. My mother was heartbroken. She had thought the doll would at least belong to both of them. Her heart seethed with jealousy and hate. She hated her uncle and was jealous of her sister. One day finding herself alone in the house she took the doll in her arms. It looked so beautiful and was so wonderful but she did not see the beauty for the hate and jealousy in her heart.

"If I can't have the doll, neither can sister," she decided. Running out into the yard she selected a rock and started beating the doll's head. Soon the pretty doll was ruined. Mother always remembered when she made the choice for wrong. She would tell us about it as she taught us to be careful with our toys, years later.

After a wrong choice is made and acted upon the harm has been done. The little girl could not bring her sister's doll back. We seldom can undo the harm when we make a wrong choice.

Aren't you happy when you have made a good choice? The satisfaction and joy is worth the taking of time to be sure you choose right.

> Life is filled with many choices
> As to what, when, where and how;
> And we need to make the right ones
> As we face them here and now.
>
> Jesus chose me for salvation
> And he's able, tried and true;
> But his choice is ineffective
> Unless I will choose him, too.
>
> Some high place I might have chosen:
> Pleasures, wealth, society;
> But one day I chose the Saviour,
> And so now He lives in me.
> —J. T. Bolding

14

Promises of
. . . Gladness

"Whereby are given unto us exceeding great and precious promises: that by these ye might be partakers of the divine nature. . . ."—II Peter 1:4

On one of those uncertain winter days I heard an ad on the television. One of the nurseries was closing out their bulbs at a very cheap price. As soon as my husband came home I asked him to go with me and buy bulbs. As we talked to the salesman he made some remarks about the day. Cold but not uncomfortable, no sunshine, "Could turn fair and it could get worse," he said.

"Well if we don't get some bulbs in the ground soon we will not have any blooms in the spring," I remarked.

"Yes, a few more days and these bulbs, as fine as they are, will be no good," he told us filling our sack generously.

A little later as my husband dug in the flower beds, under my supervision, of course, we were talking.

"We are planting promises for spring."

"Yes, and they are good and beautiful promises, but if we had not gone today they might have been too dried up and the weather too bad for planting." He held up one already showing a green tip.

The Word of God is filled with promises, wonderful promises for all occasions. Promises of comfort, promises in time of sorrow, promises of strength in hours of trial and temptation, promises of light for dark days, all these and many more are to be found for the looking and reading.

One day a lady was expecting company. She talked to her small son and asked him to be especially nice while the company was in their home.

"If you will be nice and mind me when I ask you to do things, I will buy you a scooter when our company leaves."

After the company left the little child came running to his mother. "Let's go get my scooter."

"Why, no, Jimmy we are not going to buy a scooter."

"But mother you promised," and Jimmy began to cry.

"Dear, you refused to go and sit on the porch when I asked you to, and you were very naughty at the table." The mother wiped a tear from her eye. "Mother was very embarrassed because you did not keep your promise to be good."

So it is with our Heavenly Father. He has promised so many wonderful things to his children. But always the fulfillment of his promises depends upon our willingness to meet the conditions under which those promises can be realized. Often like naughty children we pout and wonder why God is better to others than to us, never stopping to ask where we have failed.

> The life that counts is lived with God;
> And turns not from the cross—the rod;
> But walks with joy where Jesus trod—
> This is the life that counts.

Most every normal person wants their life to count for something or with somebody. Yet we so often forget the promise given in II Corinthians 9:6, "He that soweth sparingly shall reap also sparingly; and he which soweth bountifully shall reap also bountifully."

Sometimes we grow weary of sowing. We feel the harvest is too far away. There are a few companions we need to take along the way of life. These companions will make the promises of God seem brighter and more easily kept.

First we want to take HOPE as our companion. Life for the Christian should be one of hope. In Joel 3:16 we read, ". . . but the Lord will be the hope of his people, and the strength of the children of Israel."

So we have the promise of hope. We have the promise that that hope will be the Lord. Then why do so many look at life as if it were always a losing battle?

Along with hope we must keep faith within our hearts. Have faith, that no matter how dark today may be, tomorrow there will be sunshine.

Jesus talking to the disciples in Mark 11:22 said, "Have faith in God."

With hope and faith in our hearts how can we fail to have joy for our portion? With joy as our portion our worries depart. Our God who promised to be our hope if we have faith in him will not fail us.

One cannot fail to get joy from just reading the promises of God. If we would make a practice of reading the Bible and marking the promises in red then we could find them quickly in time of stress.

We must beware of false promises. Every promise in the Bible will be fulfilled if we carry out the conditions. Life is often filled with people who make promises quickly but have no thought of carrying them out.

When you write a check at the grocery store or any other place you are making the promise that the money is in the bank to cover the check. Standing in a discount store waiting to be checked out I saw a long list of names fastened on the wall. At the top were the words, "People whose checks are no good."

Many a young girl has listened to the sweet promises of her lover only to have him break his word and leave her in shame and disgrace. Promising young men have had their lives shattered because they listened to some promise of a promoter, only to find, too late, the promises were false.

65

While I was writing on this chapter the postman came and I was overjoyed to find a letter from my granddaughter. Reading her letter I thought, "She is a sweet promise of a fine good woman to come."

Then immediately for no reason I remembered the bulbs planted a few days ago. I must take time to water them or they will never come up and fulfil their promise of pretty flowers.

Children and grandchildren are the sweetest promises we can imagine but if they are to fulfil their purpose in life, we must take care to water and cultivate the best traits in them.

PROMISES

God's Word has precious promises
   He's waiting to fulfill
With gladness, hope and confidence,
   To those who do his will.

If faithfully obedient
   You walk with trusting heart,
His blessed presence will not fail,
   Nor from your life depart.

God's promises are always sure;
   On them you can depend;
They'll give your life a happy song
   And all your way attend.
               —J. T. Bolding

15

Victory Brings
. . . Gladness

*". . . So David went and brought up the Ark of God
from the house of Obededom into the city of David with
gladness."—II Samuel 6:12b*

When I was a school girl I can remember how vital it was
for our ball teams to win. When we won there would be a big
bonfire. Some people lost valuable trash and a few not so
valuable outhouses. It did not seem wrong to the school
kids. We were celebrating our victory.

David and his warriors came home rejoicing in the fact
that they had again gained possession of the Ark of God.

There are many battles we have to face in life. Many
battles of daily life will be victories if we have God's presence
with us. To David and his people the Ark of God represented
God's presence with them.

When Moses was facing the Red Sea, with the great host
of people he was leading, the picture looked dark. God gave
the orders to go forward. Sometimes going forward looks im-
possible but God's command is to go forward. He will give
the victory when we obey the orders.

Sometimes the battle of doing our duty seems a hard one

to fight, yet we are to go forward in doing our duty. The victory will be ours with God's help.

One day a woman, trying to be funny, said, "Maybe God let man invent spaceships so he would have a way to get to heaven quick when the end of time comes."

We do not need a spaceship. Jesus said: "I am the door: by me if any man enter in he shall be saved" (John 10:9).

He also said: "I am the Way, the Truth, and the Life: no man cometh unto the Father, but by me" (John 14:6).

Christ is in heaven now. When we leave this earth we will know a victory over death. We will need no spaceship to take us to glory. Our Lord will be ready to receive us, and we know we will be like Him.

> I need the influence of thy grace,
>   To speed me in my way;
> Lest I should loiter in my race,
>   Or turn my feet astray.

Children and young people especially like to enter contests. All people are in the greatest contest of all when they run the race of life.

The little pie baking contest or feats of sport are not vitally important, whether we win or loose; but the race of life is of eternal consequence.

In 1 Corinthians 15:55, 57 we read Paul's opinion of victory over death. "O death, where is thy sting? O grave, where is thy victory? . . . But thanks be to God, which giveth us the victory through our Lord Jesus Christ."

Paul expected to win the race of life. He expected his victory to be a happy time. Are we planning to win? Are we just drifting along taking the easiest way out?

Four of my grandchildren belong to the Four H Clubs. They are constantly entering contests of one kind or another. More often than not they win some kind of recognition. One day I asked the oldest about her prize.

"I expected to win, I worked hard to win."

If even school children plan and expect to win, shouldn't

we work hard and expect to win a victory in the game of life? God has promised a crown and a robe to all who win. If children will work hard to win blue ribbons, shouldn't we be willing to strive to win the crown of life?

Think of Job, an outstanding example of winning in spite of great trials. Job did what was right regardless of the fact that he seemed to be beaten.

As a college girl I heard a speaker from a foreign land make this statement: "The thing I like about Americans is that they are like rubber balls; the harder they fall the higher they bounce."

Through the many years since, I have often felt the need of bouncing, and by determining to try, have won victories.

The one thing that sustained Job and made him able to stand his trials and win a victory was the fact: "He careth for you."

We never go through trials or tribulations alone. God loves his children and always cares for them. The sad thing in life is that too many times when we have won a victory financially or in some popular project, we forget to be grateful to the one who made that victory possible.

If you think you are beaten, you are;
  If you think you dare not, you don't.
If you'd like to win, but think you can't,
  It's almost a cinch you won't.
If you think you'll lose, you're lost,
  For out in the world we find
Success begins with a fellow's will;
  It's all in the state of mind.

If you think you're outclassed, you are;
  You've got to think high to rise.
You've got to be sure of yourself before
  You can ever win a prize.
Life's battles don't always go
  To the stronger or faster man;
But soon or late the man who wins
  Is the one who thinks he can.
                                    —Anonymous

16

Serve the Lord with
. . . Gladness

"Serve the Lord with gladness: come before His presence with singing."—Psalm 100:2

Two women were talking after church about a sale which was going to start the next day.

"Oh, I wish I could go. Just my luck I must attend a missionary meeting." Her face looked long and tragic.

"Couldn't you skip it tomorrow?" the friend asked.

"Oh no, I am the leader."

Are we serving the Lord with gladness or are we just filling in until our term of service is over?

Why should we serve the Lord?

We have been bought with a price (I Corinthians 6:20; 7:23).

We belong to Him (Mark 9:41)

We have ability, we should use it (Titus 2:14).

The first time I saw the Atlantic Ocean happened to be a day when a great number of sailboats were on the water. Some were going one way, some another.

"How do they make the boats go east or west?" I inquired.

"Why it is the set of the sails which guide the boats," my companion told me.

The purpose of our salvation was that we might serve Christ. We set our sails for service or we merely drift with the breeze.

God had a plan for the salvation of the lost. That plan cost Christ a great amount of suffering but He stayed true to the course God had set out for the salvation of the world.

Christ is worthy of our service. He gave himself that we might have eternal life.

While on earth He did not live a life of ease. He went about serving others. He was disturbed from sleep to calm the storm. He paused in his preaching to feed the multitudes. He had time to heal the lame, to cleanse the leper, and to bring the dead back to life.

We go about saying, "I haven't time."

What should be the nature of our service? Faithfulness!

I observed two classes in a Sunday School. They started out the year with the same enrolment. One teacher was not brilliant or outstanding but he was faithful. His pupils knew he would be in his place when they arrived. The other teacher was much better educated, better off financially, even more attractive looking, yet he did not think anything about being absent for weeks at a time. One class grew and the boys were happy; the other dwindled away until only two were left at promotion time.

Service should be sacrificial. We have almost lost the meaning of sacrifice in this prosperous land of ours.

A man visiting in a foreign land saw a farmer and his son ploughing without oxen. They were taking turns being yoked to the plough.

"See that man?" the missionary asked. "He sold his oxen to help build our small church."

The visitor was ashamed. "I did not know what sacrifice was."

Too many of us are like the small girl who wanted to make a sacrifice for Christ. "I will do without soap and save the money for missions."

"That might not be a sacrifice since you hate to be washed

with soap," her mother admonished. "If you want to do without candy for a month, you would be making a sacrifice."

In II Samuel 24:18-25, we have the story of David refusing to offer a sacrifice which had cost him nothing.

We think we have made a real sacrifice when we leave the warm fireside and go to services on a bitter winter day.

Serve the Lord with gladness. A young Christian is often very happy serving the Lord, then like a young husband he grows tired. Most young married people enjoy doing things for each other. Later, after the new has worn off, they complain when asked to do a favor. Christians, like really happy married people, should find serving the Lord, "Sweeter as the years go by."

Our service should be consecrated. We must be willing for God to use all we have in His service. The widow who used the last of her oil to cook for the prophet received in return all she could use.

The little boy who gave up his lunch for the use of others still had a feast that day.

One of my husband's first pastorates was in a small West Texas town. The town boasted no hotel but the church members always made the pastor and his family welcome in their homes. We were students and drove ninety miles to the church on weekends.

Suddenly there was an oil boom in our little town. Every available spare room in the town was rented for very high prices, and there was no room for the pastor and his family.

We arrived in town ready to start our weekend of visiting. What a surprise! People were changed overnight. Some were dreaming of riches on their poor farms; some had already sold royalties enough to start new homes.

After we had worked all day and had no place to stay, we were about to start the long drive back home. A deacon and his wife told us we must come and spend the night with them. They lived in a three-room house and had no modern conveniences. We spent many week ends with them that winter. Their children would sleep on the floor in order for us to have a bed. I like to think God blessed that family because they shared what they had with a poor student pastor. Today they have a comfortable modern home. Their children are college graduates and have good jobs.

Our service in order to bring gladness should be whole-hearted. Women and men, too, will put all the energy and pep they can get into a project for their favorite club. Christians could change the world overnight if every Christian, at one time, really made an effort to win a lost person.

SERVICE

No service in itself is small;
  None great though earth it fill;
But that is small that seeks its own,
  And great that seeks God's will.

Then hold my hand, most gracious God,
  Guide all my goings still;
And let it be my life's one aim,
  To know and do thy will.
                    —Anonymous

17

The Bread of Life Brings
. . . Gladness

*". . . that he might make thee know that man doth
not live by bread only, but by every word that proceed-
eth out of the mouth of the Lord doth man live."*
—Deuteronomy 8:3

One night at a church supper I was amazed to see a little,
scrawny boy about ten with five hot rolls on his plate.

"What a waste," I said to myself. "He can't possibly eat
that many."

Looking at his plate a little while later I noticed he had
eaten everything on it.

Now that little boy is a grown young man. He is large
and handsome. He needed all the food he ate as a youngster
to make his body grow.

Wouldn't it be wonderful if Christians would over-read
in their Bible study. In a few years we would see great handsome young men and women in a spiritual sense.

The Bible is the textbook of the Christian. We must study
this textbook if we would know better the one about whom
it is written.

John 6:35, reads, ". . . I am the bread of life: he that
cometh to me shall never hunger; and he that believeth on
me shall never thirst."

The Bible from beginning to end is centered around the coming of Christ. Christ came and revealed the love of God. His coming revealed the nature of God and the plan for our salvation.

How can we know the way, the truth and the light unless someone tell us—unless we read and study the truths of God's word.

II Timothy 3:16, "All Scripture is given by inspiration of God, and is profitable for doctrine, for reproof, for correction, for instruction in righteousness."

The Bible is not only inspired but it is enduring. Men for hundreds of years have sought to make newer and better translations.

In about 1378, John Wycliffe started what became the first completed version of the Bible in the English language. He worked very hard to complete this translation in approximately three years. Wycliffe's Bible was a great achievement in Bible history. He was bitterly persecuted because of it and eventually died from the strain.

A little over a hundred years later a boy was born in England named John Tyndale. He longed to see the Bible available even to the farm children of his country. He was forced out of his native country, and had to live in Hamburg. Under great hardships and trials he still worked on his translations. At last he was tied to a stake and his body burned, his last words were, "Lord, open the King of England's eyes."

God heard and answered his prayer. How can we call ourselves God's children and neglect to read and study the Bible, secured for us at such great cost and sacrifice.

The Bible is not a book to be worshiped but a book to bring us to the one who is "The bread of life."

The world today is different from what it was when the Bible was written, yet the Bible will tell us how to solve any of our modern day problems if we read and study it. Every outstanding Christian feeds on the study of the Bible.

We live in an age of hurry and bluster, yet how great the

blessings of those who find some time each day to read and study.

In a special service the leader called for the one who had been going to our Sunday School longest to stand. That person had been working in the church for almost half a century. Asked later if he did not get tired of studying and teaching the same old stories he replied, "The truths of the Bible are never old. One never reads far without seeing some new truth or meaning."

MY BIBLE

Book of all Books! Book divine!
All and always thou art mine,
From beginning through to end,
I may still on thee depend;
Infidels still love to scout thee;
Critics high breed doubts about thee;
Devils low would gladly route thee,
If they could—thou Book sublime!

Jesus Christ, the Holy One,
God's all wise eternal Son,
He who at twelve years of age
Taught the book to Jewish sage—
Found no "myth" in Jonah story,
Found in Job no "Allegory,"
But with light shed down from glory
Found Himself, throughout it all!

Then to Jesus let us look,
To interpret His own book,
He who said, and also willed,
"Every jot shall be fulfilled."
Knew 'twas Heaven's revelation,
Never questioned "inspiration."
Ever taught its close relation
To Himself—Blest Book of mine!
                              —Charles D. Meigs

The Word of God has been described in the Bible as being:
Light, Psalm 119:105
Fire, Jeremiah 23:29

Seed, Luke 8:11
Bread, Deuteronomy 8:3
Milk, I Peter 2:2
Gold, Psalm 19:10
Sword, Hebrews 4:12

If you own a Bible you have a responsibility to read and study it, to teach it to others, to believe it, for it will reward you with happiness and gladness.

18

Telling the Story Brings
. . . Gladness

*And they, continuing daily with one accord in the
temple, and breaking bread from house to house, did
eat their meat with gladness and singleness of heart,
Praising God, and having favor with all the people."*
                                    —Acts 2:46, 47

TRUE WITNESS

The Lord intends for me to treat
    The needy as a brother,
And gives a task for me to do
    Which will not fit another.

It is my special privilege,
    In spite of my unfitness,
To tell men what He's done for me
    And be his faithful witness.

Now if I blind my stubborn eyes,
    And fail to help the needy,
I'll show through gross ingratitude
    That I am mean and greedy.

Oh help me, Lord, to live aright,
    My sin always confessing;
And help my witness to the lost
    To tell of Jesus' blessing.
                    —J. T. Bolding

If you truly have a joy in your soul because you are a child of the king, it should be a joy for you to tell others. If your heart is right with God and your daily life shows it, people will listen when you tell them the story of Jesus' love. If you are willing to try to witness, God will give you the words to say.

I have heard many stories told by church workers who were discouraged while visiting. They would decide to give up and go home; then they would decide to make just one more visit. That one more visit often proved a fruitful one and a blessing.

At Thanksgiving time a man was taking baskets around to the needy families. He was assisted by his ten year old boys Sunday School class. They had finished their list and gone back to the church to report.

"Would you mind going just one more place?" the pastor asked. "A call came in about a widow with three children who greatly needs help."

"We will be glad to go," the teacher and the boys said.

"It is almost night and I feel sure we will have no more calls. Why don't you take all we have left to this widow." The pastor began filling a large basket.

When the teacher and the boys drove up in front of the run-down little house they saw a boy their own age, sitting on the steps. His head was down on his arms and his shoulders were shaking with sobs.

"Here, son, what is wrong?" the man asked as he lifted out a big basket and started up the walk.

"Oh, oh, mother." The boy jumped up when he saw the visitors. "God is not dead, God is not dead!"

The mother came to the door. Two smaller children pushed out ahead of her.

"We came to bring you a Thanksgiving basket."

"I am so glad." Tears came to the mother's eyes. "You see Jimmy has been sitting on the steps and praying all day for God to send us some food for tomorrow."

"I told mom I would never believe in God again if he

couldn't hear an all-day prayer." Jimmy had dried his tears and a big grin spread over his face.

"God is never dead, son." The teacher put his arm around the boy. "Sometimes the people he wants to carry out his work are slow."

Has some child or some family suffered and been caused to doubt because we failed to witness in the right way?

Come and follow Jesus,
Serve the Lord today;
Let us walk together
In his glorious way.
—J. T. Bolding

Jesus said, "Take up thy cross and follow me."

Most churches have some plan for witnessing to the unenlisted and the lost. If we are true children of God we will want to co-operate with our church plan.

Jesus in the New Testament sent the workers out two by two. That plan is still hard to beat. Paul counted it an honor and a privilege to work and witness for the Master. Sometimes we stand and whine when asked to do something. Why can't we count it a joy to serve.

If we are willing to co-operate, if we count it a blessed privilege, we will find time to pray and study before we start. I find it is useful to keep a prayer list along with my visitation list.

A soldier would not think of going into battle without a weapon. A visitor always needs to carry a New Testament or a Bible. You may know all the Scriptures from memory but people like to see for themselves that it is in the printed word.

There are people who work a lot and never have a time when they can go from house to house visiting. How can they witness? They can talk about Christ to those they meet in their daily work. We talk about the ball games, and the weather. Why can't we talk about the vital subject of eternal life.

"So then every one of us shall give account of himself to God."

Nothing we say or do will count for much if we do not strive to keep our own lives pure and upright before men.

TELL ME THE STORY OF JESUS

Tell me the story of Jesus,
    Write on my heart every word;
Tell me the story most precious,
    Sweetest that ever was heard.

Tell how the angels, in chorus,
    Sang as they welcomed His birth,
"Glory to God in the highest!
    Peace and good tidings to earth."

Tell of the cross where they nailed Him,
    Writhing in anguish and pain:
Tell of the grave where they laid Him,
    Tell how He liveth again."

Love in that story so tender,
    Clearer than ever I see;
Stay, let me weep while you whisper,
    Love paid the ransom for me.
                        —Fanny J. Crosby

Fanny Crosby was blind and could not go about visiting or witnessing from house to house, yet she found a way to tell the story for many many years to many people.

God has a way for you to tell the story. The world waits to hear. Find the best way for you but never neglect to tell others.

19

Sacrifice Brings
. . . Gladness

"The Jews had light, and gladness, and joy, and honor."—Esther 8:16

We find in the book of Esther how gladness came to a whole group of people. Gladness came to many because one woman was willing to sacrifice her pride and her life, if necessary, to save her people.

History is filled with stories of people who were willing to sacrifice their comfort and even their lives for a cause. Joan of Arc or the Maid of Orleans, as she was called, is a notable example of a person willing to sacrifice her life for her country.

Martin Luther was willing to stand firm for his convictions. He was the leader of a Protestant reformation in Germany. He wrote many letters and sermons helping to influence people for a new way of thinking.

In our present day we see the majority of people so wrapped up in themselves they have lost sight of sacrificing for any cause or any people.

Willingness on the part of the beautiful queen Esther brought great joy to all her people.

Most of us are just common every day people and we feel

there are no outstanding sacrifices for us to make. Yet what a sad lonely place this world would be if it were not for the day to day sacrifices we see being made. A mother lives to make her family happy; a father likes most to be able to furnish the food and clothes his children need. A lover will go without lunch to buy a trinket for the one he loves.

Look about you and you will find that the happy people are the ones who gladly sacrifice for others.

Many young college students go out as summer missionaries. Some are paid by their churches but many go to help start missions and churches, working to pay their own expenses.

Two young men from very comfortable homes went to the far north. They found there a struggling little church, very much in need of help. One of the young men led the songs and one taught the junior age children. The first few weeks they could find no work and were about to be forced to return home.

"I think you can get work in the seed company," the pastor of the church told them. "It is hard but will pay enough for you to stay."

So the boys spent eight hours a day at hard work in the seed company. They spent many of the other hours painting Sunday School rooms, varnishing an old piano, and visiting for the church.

When time for the boys to go home came there were tears of gratitude shed by the members of the church. "Please come back next summer," they begged.

"That was really a lark for those boys," a woman in their home town said, unthinkingly.

Was it a lark? No, they made a sacrifice to go so far from home and work so hard. True, it was a sacrifice of mother's home cooking, of playing tennis and going swimming, attending parties. Just the same, summer fun is important to young people. They matured as Christians during the summer spent helping a small church.

The first Sunday they returned home I saw the glow on

their faces as they talked about the little church so far away. They told with love about the people they had helped enlist. The glow shining from within their hearts was reflected on their faces. The good they accomplished will live on and on through eternity.

Too many church members are sitting like empty buckets waiting to be filled. They would know real joy if they would only learn to serve. I heard of a church where the people were asked to turn in all the little, and big, complaints they had to a committee.

How sad to know only the folly of complaining, when all the blessings of God are to be had if those church members would only be willing to serve, to live for winning others to Christ.

The world would be a different place if every church member minimized his trials and magnified God's goodness.

SACRIFICE

Some feel it is a sacrifice
    To send a child to school
But still obey the law which says
    Attendance is the rule.

It really is a privilege
    To minister to needs,
To render simple kindnesses
    And do unselfish deeds.

Now Jesus truly sacrificed
    When He came down to earth,
And died for me on Calvary's tree,
    That I might have rebirth.

And now, He calls on me to die
    To sin and self each day,
And be a "living sacrifice"
    To point men on His way.

                    (Romans 12:1)
                    —J. T. Bolding

20

There Is Work to Do for
. . . Gladness

*"The hope of the righteous shall be gladness: but the
expectation of the wicked shall perish. The way of the
Lord is strength to the upright: but destruction shall be
to the workers of iniquity."—Proverbs 10:28, 29*

Are you prone to "let George do it";
　Do you idly watch and wait
While another lifts the burden
　Which the Lord placed at your gate?

Our churches are full of people who refuse to do the something they can do for the Lord. If they can't be the biggest
boulder in the mountain they will not be on the mountain
at all.

How long would many men hold their jobs if they worked
for their bosses like they work for God?

There's a task for you awaiting;
There is work for you to do;
Willingly, just glance about you;
He, your job will lead you to.

I asked a friend why he spent so much more time doing
extra things for his employer than he spent for the Lord's
work.

"Well, you see I have to depend on my employer for daily bread," he told me.

Perhaps he forgot that he must depend on God for the strength and health to carry on that daily job. Perhaps he forgot that it was God who gave him the job in the first place.

> Why not stop your hesitating;
> Throw excuses to the wind,
> As you cease your lazy waiting
> And beneath your load you bend?

It is natural for people to work harder when they have an incentive for work. Many young men, before they marry, drift from job to job and seem uninterested in their work. Let those same young men get married and start families and they have an incentive for work.

Many young converts often work harder at winning the lost than they do after they grow older. Young or old, work for the Lord will fill our hearts with gladness. Every Christian should feel a basic responsibility for the Lord's work. True, we cannot all be the tallest trees in the forest but when you walk through the woods don't you enjoy seeing the humble little violet struggling to bloom in the shade?

When a couple marries, the man accepts the responsibility of providing for his wife; the wife accepts the responsibility of making a home. They are usually happy when each works at his task. When one shirks responsibility there is unhappiness and sorrow.

When we trust Christ and become children of the King and joint heirs with the Son, we take on the task of working to bring others into his kingdom. If we refuse to work and fill our place, we are unhappy.

I have observed two kinds of church members: those who feel called into the Lord's vineyard just to eat grapes, and those who feel called to pick up a hoe and go to work making the vineyard grow. Examine yourself and if you are ashamed of what you find, pick up a hoe and go to work.

A small church started an addition to their building.

Having little money the members decided to do the work themselves. Each Saturday the men worked with saws and hammers, while the women prepared lunch for all. Great progress was made the first few months but gradually one by one the men began to make excuses and were absent on work days. Only a faithful few were left to complete the building.

It is easy to work when every one is enthusiastic and excited about some task. When enthusiasm wanes a task is hard to finish.

Washing cars is popular among the young people of our city as a means of raising money for special projects. They meet at some prominent place, put up a big sign and try to wash all the cars possible. Early in the morning there is much fun and enthusiasm. By afternoon many grow tired and find something calling them elsewhere.

Whatever the task, we find people usually do the things they want to do. The big problem is to make them want to work for the Lord.

Many parents fail to teach their children to work. "Oh, she will have to work enough later in life," a mother often says.

That mother is making a mistake. Every child has a right to be taught obedience, order, and work. True, we want our children to have fun as they grow up. On the other hand we need to teach them the fact that there is work to be done.

A family I know with five children, a working father and mother, all get off to school on time with beds made and dishes washed. How? Each child has a specific task to perform. Each is expected to accomplish that task and be dressed on time. I consider theirs one of the happiest families I know.

In God's work it is the same. A church family is much happier if each member is responsible for a task and is made to feel that he is necessary to the well-being of the church.

A family is usually unhappy when one does all the work. A church is unhappy when a small group does the work and the others merely sit and watch.

Many who are considered fine people like to sit back and never take a part, giving a generous check once in a great while. The checks are wonderful and good but every Christian should find some way to bear fruit for the Master.

"The only place where success comes before work is in the dictionary."

Work brings rewards. There is the sweet joy of fellowship. Men, whose sons grow up well-adjusted and giving no trouble, are the ones who find things to do with them. They build things or go places together, or even just work on the family car or yard together.

Did you ever hear of a small boy saying: "I don't want to help my dad on a project; my hands are too small."

Yet we so often hear Christians refuse to work for God by saying, "I just haven't the talent." In other words, "I am too small to help my Father."

Work brings self-respect. When we perform a task we are asked to do, we feel a glow of self-respect and confidence.

As children get joy from trying to achieve tasks, so Christians will rejoice if they try. An effort brings a blessing. An effort brings growth and stronger faith in our ability to accomplish something worthwhile.

Rachel Ball wrote:

> You don't need a pulpit, you don't need a pew;
> For wherever you go, there's work to do—for Jesus.

21

Seek and Find
. . . Gladness

"For the Lord shall comfort Zion: he will comfort all her waste places; and he will make her wilderness like Eden, and her desert like the garden of the Lord; joy and gladness shall be found therein, thanksgiving, and the voice of melody."—Isaiah 51:3

Would you like to be rich?

Certainly you would. People are always dreaming of suddenly becoming wealthy. Very few find this dream coming true unless they go out and work to make it come true.

Would you like to be very rich, with riches no one could steal or take away from you?

In my files I have a clipping from an old newspaper, telling the story of a man who spent most of his life seeking a buried treasure. The treasure is supposed to be gold and silver buried by the Spanish in the early days of our country.

Almost everyone is seeking something in this world. In our hectic days of hurry and competition many seek just a few moments of quiet.

To want to be rich is not in itself evil. There have been some very famous rich men who made the world a better place. They used their wealth wisely. In James 2:23 we read, ". . . and he was called a friend of God."

Job was a very righteous man yet he was extremely wealthy (Ezekiel 14:14).

Joseph of Arimathea was rich and honored, yet he loved Jesus and had the honor of placing Christ's body in a new tomb.

So we know from these examples it is not evil to be rich. It is evil to love money, to put the acquiring of wealth above more worthwhile things.

Think of the wealth we can all acquire. In II Corinthians 8:9, we read, "For ye know the grace of our Lord Jesus Christ, that though He was rich, yet for your sakes He became poor, that ye might through his poverty be rich."

If Christ has forgiven your sins you have a rich blessing no one can steal from you. You have eternal life to look forward to.

One of my college professors was asked about his new son-in-law. "Well, he hasn't much money in the bank but he has a black land farm in his head."

When I pay the life insurance premiums each month I sometimes think, "We have very little money in the bank but we have the promise of making someone well off when we die."

When one of my grandsons was five years old he came for a visit from a distant state. Since it was his first visit for any length of time, we worked hard to make his every wish come true.

"Do you like your granny?" my husband asked him one day.

"Oh yes, she will get me anything I want."

He felt he had found Christmas in July. You can truly have your prayers answered, your needs met if you trust Christ. Matthew 21:22 reads, "And all things, whatsoever ye shall ask in prayer, believing, ye shall receive."

Isn't it wonderful to think about the riches of having our faith in Christ. We might spend our lives digging in old tunnels and never even find a very pretty rock, but if we seek God's blessings and love, we are rich indeed.

When a young father and mother feel the arms of their own little baby reaching around their neck they feel a richness bought only with love.

When a child of God, in time of need, feels God's everlasting arms upholding and keeping him, he has a wealth not bought with money.

A speaker once asked a large group of people if they would like to become rich. All but four answered yes.

When asked, why, they answered as follows:

"I would have nothing left to work for."

"Things earned by the sweat of the brow are enjoyed more."

"People would always be asking me for donations."

"Money makes problems and I dislike problems."

In my lifetime I have known many people I counted rich with God's love and blessings. None of the answers of people who did not want to be rich with money could apply to them.

The more they worked for the Lord the happier they were. They always counted all their blessings as gifts from God and thanked Him for them. Their greatest joy came from being able to help others have a happier life.

In the early 1920's we were having a struggle with our family finances. My father was going to college and supporting a wife and three children at the same time. We would get so hungry for candy. Our mother would make a sorghum molasses candy. In order for the candy to be good it had to be "pulled." The pulling was as much fun as the eating. We would have contests seeing who could pull theirs the whitest. Once in awhile the candy would not be quite cool enough when impatient little hands started to pull. Then we would find ourselves in a fix, with sticky goo all over our hands and sometimes on our clothes.

Our experience with sticky hands reminds me of the rich young ruler. Mark 10:22 (Phillips Translation) tells us, "At these words his face fell and he went away in deep distress, for he was very rich."

His riches kept him from obtaining the coveted eternal life. His life was all sticky and entwined with his fortune. He could not willingly free himself of his wealth.

SEEK AND FIND

Some men find gladness in riches
Some look for it in fame;
Some men receive it in pursuing
Some Idea which makes a great name.

Some sell their souls just for pleasure
Some think peace the most worthwhile
While some find great joy in achieving
And others think only of dressing in style.

A few find real joy in their service
When rendered to those who're in need;
Doubt you they're the ones who find gladness
Which truly is gladness indeed?

—J. T. Bolding

22

Make Life Sing with
. . . Gladness

*"Ye shall have a song, as in the night when a holy
solemnity is kept; and gladness of heart, as when one
goeth with a pipe to come into the mountain of the
Lord, to the Mighty one of Israel."—Isaiah 30:29*

"She is always smiling," I said to the aunt of a very pretty
young girl. We were spectators as the girl and her friends
were rehearsing for her wedding.

"Why shouldn't she always smile," the aunt replied. "She
and the boy both were born with a silver spoon in their
mouths."

Does it take a silver spoon in the mouth to make people
sing with gladness? Some of the people who are most miserable have the most money.

Happiness is in the heart, not the bank account. A friend
of mine said, "Money makes being miserable a little more
comfortable."

In comparison with the young couple who had both known
only plenty all their lives I am thinking of a family in one
of our first pastorates.

They were eight in all. Two older girls and four younger
children of both sexes. The two older girls went away to a

State Teacher's College and worked as maids to pay their way through school. The four little ones were never clean—except maybe a little on Sunday. They played like wild Indians all around the neighborhood. People were always laughing about them and any kind of mischief was just automatically blamed on them. They had real good ears and when their mother opened the door of the old wood-burning stove to take out the huge pan of hot biscuits they usually rushed indoors and were soon at the table. The biscuits were always served with sorghum molasses or jelly made from grapes and plums gathered during the summer months off the creek banks. I have yet to meet a family happier than they. They never complained about their lack of this or that. They were happy with each other.

As a young minister and his wife ate often at that table they, too, learned some of the joy that comes from just being with the ones you love—the joy of just telling little tales of the little happenings in the community. Life can sing with gladness if we listen for the song.

When my own children were small we lived in a medium-sized city and attended a seminary. On the weekends we drove out several miles to my husband's church. The members were very good to us and we were as happy as larks. To reach our church we drove past some of the most beautiful homes in the city. A member of our country church was a governess in one of the fine homes. Sometimes she would bring large boxes of clothing and pass them out to relatives and friends. I was at times glad to be one of the friends. The clothes were very expensive and nice, just things her mistress wanted out of her way.

"They must be terribly happy to have so much money and such a lovely home," I said to her on one of her Sundays off.

"Oh no, they live in mortal fear all the time." She shook her head sadly. "They are afraid of kidnapers. They have lights all around their place shining all night, besides having a full time watchman. I am never allowed to let the children out of my sight when I am on duty."

"Maybe I have not realized what a happy life we have," I said, thinking of my own children and the fun they had walking back and forth to school.

"They are more content and love each other more than some other families with great wealth," she told me. "But they can't quite be free to laugh and live unafraid."

Since knowing that governess I have never envied the rich very much.

Joy and happiness in all times have been expressed with singing and music. The Negro field hands often sang spirituals as they picked cotton. How well I remember hearing my mother sing as she churned the butter in an old crock churn! She did not sing songs you would hear on a juke box. They were songs such as, "Shall We Gather at the River?" or "What a Friend We Have in Jesus." It was a comfort and joy to children playing near by as we heard our mother sing about the good things in life.

A man I knew as a child would always sit and listen when a group gathered around the piano to sing.

"Come on, Uncle Bill, and sing," someone would say.

He always replied, "I have a singing heart but I can't carry a tune. I'll pat my foot while you sing and play."

Ephesians 5:19 says, "Speaking to yourselves in psalms and hymns and spiritual songs, singing and making melody in your hearts to the Lord."

As Christians our lives should make beautiful melody and harmony. As Christians we should have hearts so filled with joy that they are singing hearts. When adversity comes the melody or harmony may be in a minor key. A real Christian with a singing heart will know that God is still on the throne and Romans 8:28 is still in effect. As we live before others in times of adversity, we often give them a right or wrong impression of Christianity.

Annie Johnston Flint is one of my favorite writers of poems. She wrote some of her most beautiful poems while she was wracked with pain. For a number of years I kept one of her poems taped to my cabinet door, just to remind me how wonderful is God's grace. Stories of some of our great hymns tell us their authors were having sorrow and difficulties when they were written. Fanny Crosby had a singing heart and in spite of blindness she blessed the world with her hymns.

We must teach our hearts to sing. The only way we can do that is by serving the one who put music into the world. There are so many ways we can serve. To each God has given His own way and all different ways are necessary to make the harmonies of joy and contentment.

A small child liked to look at people's pictures in the paper. She could tell when the picture was of a bride or a ball player. One day she saw the picture of a very pretty lady. "Mommie, what did this lady do?"

The mother read the article. "Dear, she died." The little girl looked at the picture awhile and then she asked a question, "How did they get her to smile like that if she is dead?"

"She smiled when she was alive and happy," the mother explained to the child.

In Isaiah 30:29 we find songs of rejoicing within the city. The Assyrians were slaughtered under its walls. The Jews were celebrating the passover memorial. This was the only festival that included a nocturnal ceremony. Each band of pilgrims on the way to Jerusalem was headed by a person who played the pipe (flute).

Today we consider music at night more enchanting than in the daytime. It brings cheerfulness to the darkness, and pleasure to the hearts.

The music in the Christian's heart makes this world a brighter, more livable place. Let's avoid ruining the harmony of our song by putting in chords of resentment, or notes of jealousy, and envy?

YOUR SONG

Now, my friend, what's the song
    Which you have in your heart?
Does it sadly drag on
    As each new day you start?

Or does joy bubble up
    As your blessings you count,
'Til your brimming-full cup
    Overflows like a fount?

You have cause to be glad?
    Then don't grumble and grouch,
Nor with countenance sad
    In some dark corner crouch.

Your glad song through the day
    Will much happiness bring
As you travel your way,
    Making joyous bells ring.

With God's love in your soul
    Sing the songs that you feel
And in Jesus' control
    Put your hands to the wheel.

Let the world hear you sing
    On life's way as you go,
And so, joyfully ring
    Out your heart's overflow.
                    —J. T. Bolding

23

Church Attendance Brings
. . . Gladness

"Glory and honor are in his presence; strength and gladness are in his place."—I Chronicles 16:27

WORSHIP

What a wonderful thing in our lives worship is,
    As on Sunday we go to the church;
And we gather with friends in the house of the Lord,
    With heads bowed, that our hearts he may search.

If within there is aught which displeases the Lord,
    He'll forgive, if we truly will ask.
Also he will endue us with strength from on high
    To perform his appointed life task.

It brings joy to my heart when we sing and we pray,
    As to Jesus' dear name we accord
With great gladness, our praise, for salvation so free,
    In the wonderful house of the Lord.
                        —J. T. Bolding

A three year old boy I know asks his mother a dozen times a week, "When will Sunday come?"

When at last she says, "When you wake up in the morning we will go to Sunday school and church," he is happy.

Wouldn't it be nice if more adults looked forward to Sunday with joy and anticipation!

Not long ago a woman from a distant state moved to our town. The church visitor called on her and urged her to attend our worship services.

"I will probably visit around in several churches after we are better settled," she glibly assured her caller.

That very afternoon the newcomer called the president of a civic club and asked how she could get to be a member. She was anxious to begin club work, but an invitation to church brought forth no spark of anticipation or joy.

JOY IN WORSHIP

Now the blessings of a friendship
Are a countless multitude,
And the joys of Christian worship
Are so great in magnitude,

That it makes me often marvel
At the thoughtlessness of men
In neglecting just to travel
To God's house each week again.

For 'tis joy to meet the brethren,
And to intermingle there
In the fellowship of Christians
Bent on worship and on prayer.
—J. T. Bolding

According to the reports in our daily newspaper, only about one-fifth of our city's population attends Sunday worship services. That one-fifth attends on pretty days or special days. It is a much sadder story on rainy or cold days.

Is it any wonder so many families and homes are broken and people are unhappy! They neglect going to the worship services where they could be bound and knit together with a chord of love. They do not claim the promise, "Glory and honor are in his presence; strength and gladness are in his place."

"Oh, I have not felt so near the Lord since I was a child,"

a friend told me after she had been to a homecoming meeting in her childhood community.

Did she feel closer to God in that small country church because the people were better? Maybe it was because she had more confidence in the ones she met there. I am afraid she had left God there many years before when she married and moved to the city. Throughout the years she had neglected to attend services and stay close to God.

Back again for a service in the old home church she remembered all the happy days of childhood when she worshiped there with her parents. Of course she felt close to God there, for there it was she had known his love and worshiped him. Neglect had caused her to spend many fruitless years.

God is near in all our worship services, whether the place be a two million dollar building on a city street or a small wooden church on a country road. He is as close to our hearts as we will allow him. It is up to each individual to draw near unto God and call upon His name.

So many parents are missing the blessing of worshiping with their children! Large city churches often must hire policemen to direct traffic before and after Sunday School. So many parents drive by the church and put their little ones out, coming back an hour later to pick them up. In the meantime they have relaxed and read the morning paper, often commenting about the serious problem of "the young folks going to the dogs."

According to the judges in our courts the problem children are the ones who grow up without ever having known the security of parents who worship God.

Do parents really get more joy out of fishing, visiting relatives, just being lazy at home, than they would from sitting in the house of the Lord and truly worshiping him?

Psalm 96:6 reads, "Honor and majesty are before him: strength and beauty are in his sanctuary."

When I was about twelve years old we moved from a village in Oklahoma to a larger town in Texas. The church we started attending had beautiful stained glass windows. I had never seen windows like those before. I attended every service. Each time I sat in a different part of the building so I could enjoy a different window. My favorite window was the one depicting Jesus holding the little lamb in his arms.

Each window had a name plate at the bottom, telling to whom it was dedicated. As a curious little girl I would read those names and think how happy the people already in heaven must be to know they had a special window.

Knowing how I loved my church as a child and as a woman, knowing I always feel God is near and gives fresh strength at the worship services, knowing the firm foundation and security I receive from attending my church, I would never want my own children to miss that blessing.

During World War II, I went to visit my Chaplain husband in Louisiana. We attended services in a one-room church building. The people made us welcome and we received strength for the ordeal of parting which was very near. Whatever your problem or your blessing, it will be more easily accepted if you have the strength found in worship.

WINGS OF WORSHIP

When the beautiful tones of the organ peal out,
   And the incense of prayer round me clings,
To the depths I am filled with God's glorious love,
   As my soul soars on worship's glad wings.

Then my heart overflows with the Spirit of God,
   And my being so joyously sings,
As the beautiful tones of the organ peal out
   And my soul soars on worship's glad wings.

—J. T. Bolding

24

Inheritance of
. . . Gladness

*"That I may see the good of thy chosen, that I may
rejoice in the gladness of thy nation, that I may glory
with thine inheritance."—Psalm 106:5*

A minister of the gospel lay dead. People came in and
out the funeral parlor. As two women were leaving one
said, "He didn't leave his children anything."

Being one of those children I began to think of all the
things he did leave his children.

How foolish those two women were!

First of all there was his good name. Wherever we went
we could always be proud of our father's good name.

True, he had been a humble man, a poor man, never own-
ing a large amount of worldly goods; but he was loved
over the countryside and respected.

> What, my friend, will you be leaving
>   For your loved ones when you're gone?
> Will a good name be their portion
>   When you have to travel on?

Will your dear ones then inherit
Temporal things that men may see;
Or will you have built within them,
Honor, truth and honesty?

—J. T. Bolding

As I sat there I remembered many things in my child-hood. One time dad had bought all of us an ice cream cone—not so much in itself, but so much in the light of the fact that he was out of work at that moment.

"The Lord knows where he wants me to preach next," he would tell us. Sure enough, soon there would be a place.

Oh, foolish woman, we inherited the memory of a happy childhood, and the memory of parents who bowed down in prayer and taught us to do the same.

Then our father left the inheritance of faith in our Heavenly Father. All my sisters and my brother were Christians from an early age. Could any inheritance be greater?

Psalm 37:11 tells us, "But the meek shall inherit the earth; and shall delight themselves in the abundance of peace."

My father left his children an inheritance of peace. We were never allowed to fight and quarrel at home and we have never found out it could be done after we left home.

Any earthly father who leaves his children the memory of seeing him live a Christian life before the world, leaves them a great inheritance.

How great the inheritance we have on this earth from Christ our Lord, who has gone away for a little while!

"My peace I leave with you."

"A comforter will come." Someone had said that God's hand is still under us and his goodness is lower than we can fall.

In Matthew 5 we are promised, "Inherit the earth."

Knowing of our great inheritance we should seek to live like heirs of the King. We should cease from growing angry. Anger causes us to loose the effectiveness of our prayers. Anger will lead to malice. We should strive never to be impatient and jealous.

I knew one son who hurried to a lawyer the day his father died to start proceedings for probation of a will.

Jesus told us what we would receive. We have only to trust and believe.

"Wisdom is better without an inheritance, than an inheritance without wisdom" (Laconics).

INHERITANCE OF . . . GLADNESS

To bestow earth's proud possessions
  On your children here below
Often makes them independent
  And away from God they go.

But you safely give them knowledge,
  Wisdom and sweet freedom too,
Of the sort your forebears handed
  Through great sacrifice to you.

Do bestow an education
  As it's taught in public schools;
But it's yours to teach of Jesus
  And his blessed book of rules.

If you help them find salvation
  And for Christ teach them to live
What a marvelous endowment!
  Oh, what gladness you will give!
                              —J. T. Bolding

25

Today's
. . . Gladness

"And behold joy and gladness, slaying oxen, and killing sheep, eating flesh, and drinking wine; let us eat and drink; for tomorrow we shall die."—Isaiah 22:13

If you were asked the question, "What would you do if you knew you had only twenty-four hours to live?" how would you answer!

Perhaps if there was an unsaved member of your family, you would want to take enough of those precious twenty-four hours to plead with that person to trust Christ. That would be the most important thing you could do, if your own heart was right with God. Most of us would have little loose ends of business we would need to tidy up for those we would leave behind.

Many years ago a member of our family made a trip across several states visiting his brothers and sisters. Just before he left each home he would tell them he loved them and would not meet them again until they met in Heaven. He had been told he had an incurable disease and would soon die. What a happy time his relatives had enjoying his visit until he came to leave.

He was an inspiration to all who knew him in those last months. He gladly explained that he was ready to meet God and had no fear.

In the spring of the year when I was a child, my mother always planted a garden. Sometimes she would lack a few rows of having everything planted. If she looked at the clouds and decided we were going to have rain, she would put everyone in the family to work finishing those few rows. When the seeds were all planted there would be plants to set out.

"Hurry before the rain starts," she would urge us. Sometimes we would get sprinkled on a little as we hurriedly pushed the tender plants into the ground.

When the garden was finished and the rain falling mother would look out the window and say, "Isn't it good to have the garden all planted and getting the benefit of this good rain?"

When our last days on earth come, are we going to spend them frivilously eating and drinking, or will we, to the very last, plant seeds for good. I wonder if we will be able to look down from heaven and see the seed coming up, growing and doing good in the world.

Very often I catch myself being envious of people who seem to have a great deal of time to spend just as they please. Yet, would I be satisfied with the harvest they will reap from their wasted time?

IT'S UP TO YOU

Life itself can't give you joy,
    Unless you really will it;
Life just gives you time and space . . . .
    It's up to you to fill it.
                        —Selected

What is life to you? Is it just time to be spent. Is it a precious gift to be used to the best advantage each day?

We visited a lady who had many fine pieces of cut glass. Everywhere one looked in her house there was some kind of cut glass, yet it did not give me the thrill it should have. There was very little sparkle to any of it; in fact it was very dusty and dirty.

We ate in another home where the lady of the house served water from a very beautiful cut glass pitcher. "My only piece of cut-glass," she explained. "So I use it as often as I can."

Do you see two kinds of lives in this little tale? Some people have many talents, lots of time and even money. Do they use them for good, to bring joy and blessings. No, it is wasted, and grows dull with dust. What should be a sparkling happy life is only dull and useless.

Then there are others who have few talents, and not much of this world's goods to give, but they sparkle and shine in the glow of usefulness to the delight of all who meet them.

Time is running out for every person alive today. How are we spending those precious moments, hours, and days?

God showed how much he loved and trusted the human race when he gave us time. The richest man in America cannot buy a minute of time. Time is the precious possession of each of us. We cannot call it back when we squander it. We cannot call it back when we use it well; we only reap the results of how we spent it.

Psalm 118:24 tells us, "This is the day which the Lord hath made; we will rejoice and be glad in it."

Today is our day. God gave it to us. Let us be glad in it.

I picked up the following poem on a card in a cafeteria. I do not know who wrote it or the kind of life the author lived. But this poem preaches a sermon all its own.

Life is a gift to be used every day
Not to be smothered and hidden away;
It isn't a joy to be sipped now and then
And promptly put back in a dark place again.

Life is a gift the humblest may boast of
And one that the humblest may well make the most of.
Get out and live it each hour of the day,
Wear it and use it as much as you may;

Don't keep it in niches and corners and groves,
You'll find that in service its beauty improves.

—Selected

Again I say, today is yours. So please don't let it slip away unused for good.

From Shakespeare's "Julius Caesar" we read:

There is a tide in the affairs of men,
Which taken at the flood, leads on to fortune;
Omitted, all the voyage of their life
Is bound in shallows and in miseries.

The way you spend today may make a difference in all the rest of your life. Will you eat drink and be gay, or will you cultivate and sow happiness and good for others?

A TIME FOR EVERYTHING

There's a time to get and a time to give,
    And a time to throw away;
There's a time to do a kindly deed,
    And that time is today.

There's a time to sing and a time to mourn,
    A time for joy and sorrow;
There's a time to love; but the time to hate
    Might better be tomorrow.

There's a time to sleep and a time to wake,
    A time for work and play;
But the time to speak an evil thought
    Passed by us yesterday.

—Frank A. Waugh